Jason Ryan Dorsey consistently delivers

Educator Comments

"Jason Dorsey has made a difference in the values _____ ___ _____ and administrators alike. They and the students of West Virginia will be challenged to establish and achieve ever higher goals as a result."

—HENRY MAROCKIE, STATE SUPERINTENDENT OF SCHOOLS
WEST VIRGINIA DEPARTMENT OF EDUCATION

"Jason knows what it takes to build a Culture of Loyalty so critical for school administrators. He showed us by example the specific actions and inspiration necessary to be agents of change for leading faculty and students."

—VIRGINIA TRCHALEK, LEADERSHIP TASB PROGRAM MANAGER
TEXAS ASSOCIATION OF SCHOOL BOARDS

"I continue to get comments from teachers, parents and administrators that what Jason said seemed to speak directly to them. He understood their needs and feelings. That is the sign of a great speaker."

—PETER ROSENSTEIN, FORMER EXECUTIVE DIRECTOR
NATIONAL ASSOCIATION FOR GIFTED CHILDREN

"*AWESOME JOB!* You 'connected' with the audience right away by using your wit and humor—never deviating from your powerful and inspirational message. Participants left feeling 'energized.' We'll definitely recommend you to other business, governmental, and educational entities. Thank you for doing such an outstanding job."

—JIM VIDAK, COUNTY SUPERINTENDENT OF SCHOOLS
TULARE COUNTY OFFICE OF EDUCATION, VISALIA, CALIFORNIA

"If you want an energetic, dynamic presenter who keeps people totally engaged, Jason Dorsey is your man. He is truly motivational and provides much food for thought!"

—YVONNE V. DAVIS, STATE DIRECTOR
CAREER AND TECHNICAL EDUCATION, MAINE DEPARTMENT OF EDUCATION

"Jason delivers a new perspective on school improvement that educators actually use! His contagious enthusiasm and humor makes his programs entertaining while content rich."

—VICKI BALDWIN, PRINCIPAL
GONZALO GARZA HIGH SCHOOL

"Jason presents a fresh perspective in a lively and enthusiastic manner. Educators at all levels and disciplines can benefit from his practical viewpoints and put his knowledge to use immediately."

— RICHARD WONG, EXECUTIVE DIRECTOR
AMERICAN SCHOOL COUNSELOR ASSOCIATION

Jason Ryan Dorsey consistently delivers results:

Educator Comments (more)

"Jason's book and live presentation are excellently planned and delivered, with enough humor to make the most exhausted participant feel relaxed and invigorated."
—JAMES M. WALKER, DIRECTOR
NATIONAL RESOURCE CENTER FOR YOUTH SERVICES

"Jason delivered outstanding programs to over 22,000 educators and students in my region. Teachers, administrators, and counselors implemented his practical strategies immediately. I strongly recommend him for your audience."
— JACQUIE CROTEAU, TECH PREP COORDINATOR, INDIANA

"Your insight on the needs and desires of today's youth and the parent/child relationship is nothing short of amazing! You inspired, renewed, and challenged us! In short, you helped ignite the 'movement for change.' "
—DA MICA L. O'BRYANT, PLANNING COMMITTEE CHAIR
GOVERNOR'S CONFERENCE FOR A DRUG FREE INDIANA

"Jason discovered his purpose in life early – inspiring people to succeed. Jason sincerely makes a difference."
—VERONICA OWENS, MEMBER OF PARLIAMENT
SECRETARY TO THE MINISTRY OF EDUCATION, COMMONWEALTH OF THE BAHAMAS

"Motivating! Inspiring! Easy to read! This book's excellent 'cookbook' approach helps the reader create a vision of their vocational future. Once the vision is created, the book details steps to achieve the reader's vision. A 'must read' not only for the young, but for anyone entering or re-entering the job market."
—VICKI WRIGHT, EXECUTIVE DIRECTOR
TEXAS JUVENILE PROBATION COMMISSION

"Jason Dorsey's *Graduate to Your Perfect Job* is indeed on target. After this book, readers certainly shall be better prepared to seek their 'perfect job.' "
—GEORGE KOZMETSKY, CHAIRMAN
Ic^2 INSTITUTE ADVISORY BOARD

"Students, parents, and educators alike cannot help but be inspired by Jason's message, integrity and humor. Jason is a true role model—he lives the message he brings to his audience. Our schools were calling Jason's office before he even left Oklahoma, trying to schedule his next visit!"
—BETTYE FINNELL, ASSISTANT DIRECTOR
SOUTHEASTERN OKLAHOMA GEAR UP PARTNERSHIP

Youth Appreciate Jason's Message:

Educator Comments

"Jason spoke to over 6,000 of our eighth- and ninth-grade students. Both of his presentations were simply outstanding. He truly inspired the students to overcome the challenges in their lives to achieve their greatest dreams. Jason has the unique ability to capture and relate to young people. I would recommend Jason Dorsey without reservation for student and educator events!"

—RON JOHNSON
ASSISTANT SUPERINTENDENT, HOUSTON ISD

"Jason has a talent that is unmatched by any other speaker. The students were focused and energized by Jason's ability to reach out and grab their attention. Our students will use his *'No More Excuses!'* message immediately in pursuing their dreams."

—MIKE MARTINEZ, PRINCIPAL
CHANNEL ISLANDS HIGH SCHOOL
OXNARD, CALIFORNIA

"Although Mr. Dorsey looks as if he would have nothing in common with our students, he connected with them immediately. He is a very energetic and charismatic young man who knows just how to speak to teenagers."

—CHARLOTTE BROWN, TECH PREP CO-DIRECTOR
FASHION INSTITUTE OF TECHNOLOGY, NEW YORK CITY

"Jason's message was an inspiration to all 2,400 of our students! He brought his story to life with each student—expertly touching emotions and situations that they are going through today."

—JERRY MORGAN, TECH-PREP COORDINATOR
LIVINGSTON, LOUISIANA

"You captivated the students and gave them excellent information and advice. We look forward to working with you again and again."

—SUSAN HANFLAND, DIRECTOR
EASTERN ILLINOIS EDUCATION FOR EMPLOYMENT SYSTEM

"Jason was unbelievable in his ability to hold the middle school students mesmerized. I have never seen a speaker that could match Jason's ability for keeping students so intently involved and for sending such a powerful message."

—CINDY MAGGIO, DIRECTOR
GEAR UP OF NORTHEAST TEXAS

Youth Appreciate Jason's Message:

Educator Comments (more)

"You did a fantastic job keeping everyone upbeat and motivated to participate. We were looking for a speaker that would appeal to a very diverse group of participants, and you fit the bill perfectly. I would happily recommend you to other communities looking to come together to build solutions to community issues. Your enthusiasm is inspiring."

—CHRISTINE RUMAN, GRANTS COORDINATOR
WATERBURY DEPARTMENT OF EDUCATION
WATERBURY, CONNECTICUT

"Thank you for your dynamic presentation! You did a wonderful job of relating to both the students and employers, and everyone was intrigued by what you had to say. We were extremely fortunate to have you as our speaker."

—RACHEL RICHARDSON, SPECIAL PROJECTS COORDINATOR
LIMA/ ALLEN COUNTY CHAMBER OF COMMERCE
LIMA, OHIO

"Your thoughts on young people, their future, and how to structure their plans to make the most of that future were so appropriate and timely. It was immediately apparent that you understand your audience and are able to relate to their current position as well as address their uncertainties about the future."

—DR. SHARON MCGAVICK, PRESIDENT
CLOVER PARK TECHNICAL COLLEGE
LAKEWOOD, WASHINGTON

"I asked the students what they got from the book. All of them unanimously stated, 'Because I read that book, I know that whatever I set my mind to I can do. And, I learned how to tie a tie.'"

—ERIKA TONSFELDT, TECH PREP COORDINATOR
OMAHA, NEBRASKA

"Jason Dorsey impacts people's lives profoundly by creating a constructive avenue for self-expression and personal success."

—RICHARD WILLIAMS, NATIONAL DECA PRESIDENT

"Jason gave one of 'the best motivational speeches' that I and many of my fellow participants had ever heard. He moved every single person in the room, literally bringing tears to the eyes of many of us. His message that it's up to each of us to put our plans into action was taken to heart by every participant from over 30 countries, as was evident by his well deserved standing ovation!"

—REINHARDT SMIT, DEPUTY PRESIDENT
THE HAGUE INTERNATIONAL MODEL UNITED NATIONS YOUTH ASSEMBLY
THE NETHERLANDS

Student thoughts about

Graduate to Your Perfect Job

"Jason taught me to stop making excuses and be responsible for my actions if I really want to succeed."

—TANA G., AGE 13

"This is the first book I've read all the way through."

—BRIAN D., AGE 15

"I got a job and a college scholarship! Thanks for making it so simple!"

—SARAH M., AGE 17

"What you said has broadened my horizons. It's hard to describe. You told me to get internships and talk to everyone I could about journalism. This summer I have an internship with *The Houston Chronicle*! Thank you! Thank you! Thank you!!!"

— SHEILA W., AGE 17

"Your book changed my life."

—JENNIFER G., AGE 15

"In just a few hours, you touched my life… Your words on reaching my goals, the value of persistence, a positive attitude, talking to people, patience, and passion helped me a lot!"

— LANCE T., AGE 16

"I have already achieved four of my goals… Thank you so much!"

— MARIA M., AGE 17

"You are someone my age who has achieved so much. You are a real inspiration to many, especially me."

— ELIZABETH K., AGE 20

"I felt like I had no future until I read Jason's book. Now I can dream big!"

—MARK V., AGE 15

"You really inspired me to think about reality, my life and my goals. I did exactly what you said and it has made a difference in my life."

— LARRY J., AGE 19

"Your story is great. Because of you I believe that if I put my mind to something and spend some time on it, I can do anything!"

— DONNA S., AGE 14

Also by Jason Ryan Dorsey

MY REALITY CHECK BOUNCED!

50 WAYS TO IMPROVE SCHOOLS FOR UNDER $50

STOPPING SCHOOL VIOLENCE STARTS WITH YOU

GRADUATE TO YOUR PERFECT JOB

Jason R. Dorsey

A LITL BOOK
Published by Golden Ladder Productions, Ltd.
Austin

LITL

Golden Ladder™ Productions, Ltd.
Post Office Box 4860
Austin, Texas 78765

First LITL Edition, 1997

Second LITL Edition, 2004

Third LITL Edition, 2008

Cover design by FODA Studio
Interior book design by Native Creative
Edited by Dee Ann Campbell
Illustrations by Mike Crixell
Author photo by Nils Juul-Hansen

Manufactured in the United States of America

Library of Congress Catalog Number 97-93471

Dorsey, Jason R.
*   Graduate to your perfect job*
*   / Jason R. Dorsey*

ISBN   0-9657725-1-9

Two people have been instrumental
in helping me find my life direction.
This book is dedicated to both of them.

To My Mother:
For teaching me that
"water seeks its own level."

To Brad Armstrong:
For teaching me that the only limits
to a person's potential are the ones
they create for themselves.

CONTENTS

FOREWORD

January 3, 2006

When I wrote the first edition of *Graduate to Your Perfect Job*, at age 18, my goal was simple: help people my age shortcut the path to real world success. I imagined one day traveling the world, working one-on-one and in large groups with young adults who were ready to get ahead. Nine years later, my dream has become reality—as your dream will when you apply the simple strategies and actions in this book.

Graduate to Your Perfect Job is different from other "how-to" books, because it's written from a young person's perspective. The examples, actions and stories are all taken from my experience navigating the sometimes confusing transition from school to the real world. Whether you are in high school, in college, or are a recent graduate, *this book spells out exactly what you can do right now to live your most fulfilling dreams*.

I know the strategies and actions in this book work, because I've seen them work in my own life. I've also received thousands of e-mails and letters from young adults around the world who have used this book to jump-start their success. These readers have started their own businesses, launched volunteer efforts, been accepted to prestigious education programs, and landed outstanding jobs.

As you apply the strategies and actions in this book, and move closer to the success you want, I have a favor to ask: please share your learning with others. Maintaining this chain of knowledge keeps society moving forward and allows you to appreciate the success you create.

Congratulations on choosing to live your real world dreams!

Your teammate,

Jason Ryan Dorsey

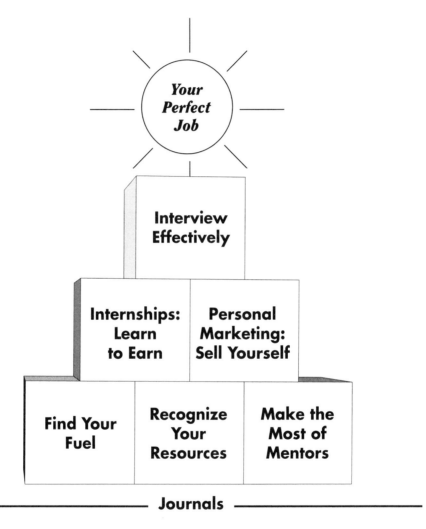

The Six Steps to Your Perfect Job

Introduction

Why Should You Listen to Me?

My name is Jason Dorsey, and as I write this I am an 18-year-old junior at The University of Texas at Austin.

You may think it is outrageous that such a young person should write a book about finding the job you want, but the advice you are about to read is based on personal experience. Here is the short version of my life and the experiences I have been granted and have created for myself. You are not me, so you will not be able to exactly follow my path. But what I absolutely believe is that you can chart a path for yourself and build the resources you need to go as far as you desire. This is how I have done it.

My family always stressed education. Growing up in Brenham—a peaceful, rural community in Central Texas—gave me strong family values and a sense of community, but did not offer all the learning opportunities available to students in larger cities. To overcome this geographical disadvantage, I began attending colleges and other programs while a sophomore in high school.

First, I attended a medical program at The University of Miami in Coral Gables, Florida. At the time, I was interested in medicine and felt that first-hand work would help me discover if it was truly the career path for me. After four weeks of meeting with terminally-ill patients, deciphering lab reports, and getting little sleep, I realized it was not. This career exploration saved me from pursuing an education and career I would not have been happy with.

I spent my junior year of high school back in Brenham, but knew that I wanted to explore archeology, something completely different from any of the paths I had previously considered. For eight weeks I sweated on an archeological dig in the Mediterranean under the instruction of Harvard University archeologists. There were two other participants my age on the dig, but the majority were graduate students. The experience combined field work and course work, with many top archeologists from around the world lecturing daily.

After such an exhilarating experience, I was not excited about returning to high school, so I applied to a program through Clarkson University in upstate New York. I was accepted into the program and "skipped" my senior year of high school to start college early.

Attending The Clarkson School enabled me to pursue my passion for business while also helping "at-risk" students with their classes. One of the students in particular, an amazing basketball player from New York City, was greatly in need of both academic and personal support. It was a life-changing experience to help him better his academic standing and clarify his views on life. I know I learned more from him than he learned from me.

Life at Clarkson was filled with setbacks and successes, and I learned from them all. I also made an important decision: No more cold weather. So, after one academic year in the snow, I decided to attend the Business Honors Program at The University of Texas at Austin (UT).

Before arriving at UT, I spent the summer working at the Fort Worth, Texas branch of Prudential Securities—a large and reputable brokerage house. Interning in a field directly related to the stock market was extremely exciting, especially since I did not have any previous work experience.

In order to get the internship, I called every brokerage house in the phone book. After a full day of phone calls, I was able to schedule a 30-minute meeting with the Prudential branch manager. I entered the meeting with enthusiasm and professional preparation. Basically, I gave him my résumé and told him I wanted to work for free!

I started the next week.

My main duty was to conduct research for various brokers on high market capitalization equities (blue chip stocks). Interning allowed me to see the often unglamorous aspects of the stock market, and helped me to gain first-hand knowledge about how companies view prospective employees. While in Fort Worth for the summer, I took advantage of all opportunities, whether striking up a conversation with a gentleman at a bookstore about stocks (who later got me in to see one of the richest people in America), or working in the evenings as a busboy to learn more about operating a restaurant from (literally) the ground floor.

While attending UT, I made strong networking connections in the internship arena. Most of the networking I accomplished was through the mail and chance meetings; it's critical to be ready to take advantage of every opportunity that comes your way. Through my persistence and consistency, I attended several office visits over the semester break (before many of my peers began to consider the employment search), met with numerous CEO's and other high-profile business leaders, and gained three mentors.

The methods outlined in this book are a compilation of the experiences I gained by contacting prospective employers and mentors, developing internship opportunities, and utilizing them to their fullest. Through my contacts and mentors' guidance and support, I realized that I have a passion, not only for business, but for networking and the job search. At the time of this writing, I have several standing offers for internships, and have received many full-time employment offers.

In mid-December 1996, I met with one of my newly acquired mentors. We were discussing our goals in life and what we wanted to accomplish, both short and long term. This particular mentor retired at a very young age and was pursuing his dreams to the fullest. He asked me what I would do if I could do anything. The more I considered this question, the clearer the answer came: I wanted to write a book. He bluntly asked, "What's keeping you from writing a book right now?" I replied, "Well, I'm too busy with school and recruiting. I don't have time to write a book. Besides, why would anyone want to read a book by me?"

His answer was a revelation. "If you want to write, write now. Write a book based on your experiences contacting mentors, recruiters, and other influential people. With your large network, experience, and ambition, you have put yourself in a position where you can conceivably get whichever job you want, right out of college. You could help a lot of people by teaching, in an easy, step-by-step manner, what you have learned from your experiences."

For the next two weeks, I spoke with several recruiters, business owners, and mentors. They all thought the idea was great, but once again I felt I did not have the time to maintain my grades in college and write this book to the best of my abilities. Then another life-directing experience fell into place.

On January 5, 1997, one of my mentors gave me a copy of *The Instant Millionaire,* by Mark Fisher. The book not only covers making money, but also centers around focusing your life goals and incorporating them into your daily activities. I read the book on January 6th and experienced a turning point in my life.

On January 7th, at 1:58 AM, I could not sleep. Thoughts about my goals and my current life path kept circling around, keeping me from falling asleep. As I lay awake, a song from my past kept running through my mind as well, reminding me of a schoolmate who let his heart lead him through life. At that moment, I got out of bed and wrote a contract to myself. In this contract, I said that since I already had sixty hours of college credit completed, I would take one semester off and write this book to the best of my abilities. It was the hardest decision I have ever made. Two-and-a-half weeks later, the first draft of the book was finished and I began to work with an editor.

In assembling this book, I not only drew on my own experiences in networking, interviewing, obtaining mentors and internships, but also on the experience of numerous recruiters, human resources personnel, and business owners. I designed the book as an all-inclusive job search manual for high school, college, and entry-level people wanting to find their perfect job.

Once I completed the manuscript, I contacted several different publishing companies and literary agents about publishing the book. They all were interested, but wanted over a year to take the book from manuscript to finished product!

Having withdrawn from school for my self-contracted one semester, this timeline did not excite me, to say the least. The only thing the publishers uniformly agreed upon was that the book could not be on store shelves before May 30, 1997, my nineteenth birthday.

Committed to getting the book out by my birthday, I devised a somewhat nontraditional route to publishing. Using and expanding my network, I assembled a team of professionals with the goal of publishing the book before May 30, 1997. *The team members were unique because they agreed to work on the project without any up-front money. They believed in what I wanted to accomplish and they wanted to be part of it.*

You are now reading a book that was written in twenty days and published in under four months.

Anyone can achieve their goals once they find the motivation within themselves to do it. I encourage you to read this book, write your goals, work the plan, and obtain the job you want. Don't set a ceiling for yourself; the sky is no longer the limit...

Your friend,

Jason R. Dorsey

P.S. Once you read the book, I would love to hear your feedback. Please feel free to pass along any ideas, comments, or experiences by writing to me at:

Jason Dorsey
P.O. Box 49648
Austin, Texas 78765

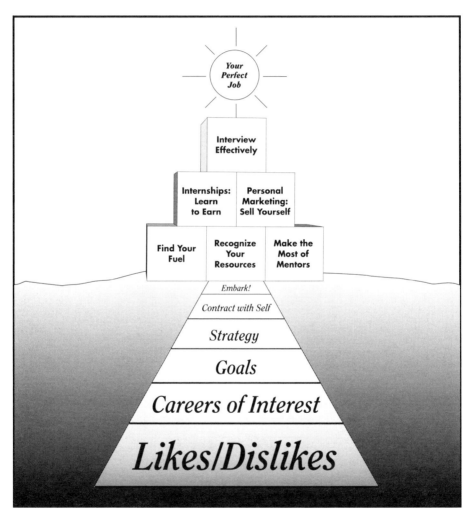

The Direct Path to Finding Your Focus

Preparation:
Focus, Focus, Focus

Finding a job is something almost everyone will do at some point in their lives, usually beginning around age sixteen. The average person can expect to change jobs a number of times before retirement. The job search is often seen as a fearful and intimidating experience, but it doesn't have to be that way. The sooner you begin creating a foundation for your future, the faster you will achieve the career you desire.

This book is designed to be a step-by-step, reader-friendly guide that covers all the bases necessary to enable a reader to obtain the job he or she *really* wants. However, depending upon your age and aspirations, it may be more appropriate for you to search for an internship to assist you in sharpening your career goals.

You may utilize each step of this book separately, but it will be most useful to you if you read it as a whole. View the job search as a process rather than a series of independent actions. Throughout the book you will be encouraged to write down your observations and data in your journal at the end of the book. While this may seem time-consuming, the information you enter now will help create opportunities for you later.

Reading this book will help you to obtain a job, an internship, and a mentor. All of these will benefit you and all lay the groundwork for a successful life. When working with the book, be honest with yourself regarding your goals and priorities; if you're not, the only person you'll be cheating is yourself. Stay focused—I know you can do it!

Determining Your Goals and Strategy

Before embarking on a journey, it is best to identify where you are going. The job search is no different. Maybe you already have an idea what you want to do with your life, or have no idea whatsoever. Whatever the situation is, you should list your job search goals.

Listing your goals is one of the most powerful things you can do to begin achieving them. Getting your goals on paper accomplishes several things: It pushes you to think through your goals and ask yourself that challenging question, "What do I really want?" Seeing them in black and white takes your dreams to a new level of reality. Now you can actually see and say what you want to accomplish in your life—and that's motivating!

There are six steps to take to begin finding your goals. The following exercise will help organize your thoughts. After reading this book and gaining more knowledge in your chosen field, you may change your mind about what you want to do. That's fine, because you won't waste time pursuing a career that won't hold your interest, and you can utilize the skills you learned to help you pursue a career that is a better fit for you.

1. Think for five minutes, then write down your:

Favorite color: _____ Personal Hero: _____

Favorite movie: _____ Favorite music: _____

Jobs of interest: _____

Jobs of no interest: _____

Annual Salary You Want: _____

Ideal city for employment: _____

Potential careers of interest (List five careers of interest to you):

I. _____

II. _____

III. _____

IV. _____

V. _____

2. If you still are unsure about any possible careers, don't worry. Get some ideas on paper and then use the strategies outlined in this book to better focus your future. As you proceed with understanding industries, interning, conducting informational interviews, and building your network, you will greatly enhance your ability to pinpoint specific careers of interest.

3. Determine your top five short-term goals (up to six months) and your top five long-term goals (2+ years). Incorporate obtaining mentors, interning, and obtaining full-time employment into these lists.

SHORT-TERM GOALS:

I. School: _____

II. Job: _____

III. Friends: _____

IV. Volunteering: _____

V. Leadership: _____

LONG-TERM GOALS:

I. School: _____

II. Job: _____

III. Friends: _____

IV. Volunteering: _____

V. Leadership: _____

4. Now you have some idea of where you want to go (direction), the next step is to determine a plan of attack (strategy). A sample plan of attack is:

GOAL: I want to have a career as a _____.
- I will write a résumé.
- I will have five professionals review my résumé.
- I will send ten letters of inquiry to prospective employers.
- I will research two companies or industries per week.
- I will conduct one practice interview this week.
- I will go on five interviews this month.
- I will get the job I *want* within six weeks from today.

5. Write a contract to yourself outlining your goals and then go into as much detail as possible regarding your plan of action to reach those goals. Sign and date this agreement and post it near your bed so you see it daily.

6. Embark on the job search journey. *You can do it!!*

Now, take a close look at your goals and your plan of attack that you wrote down. Are they aligned? Will your strategies enable you to reach your goals?

For example, if your goal for your first semester in college is to get a 4.0 GPA, and your plan of attack is to party four days per week and study thirty minutes per day, it will be very difficult to reach your goal. By changing your plan of attack to studying three hours per day and partying only one night per week, you will have a greater chance of achieving your goal.

Your plan should detail how you will fulfill your priorities and achieve your goals. Make it as detailed as possible, and set goals to judge your performance as you continue on your plan of attack. Included in your plan of attack should be the job you want and how it fits within your long-term goals. Having great goals and no plan of attack is like saying you're going to make money without taking action. It does not happen.

UNDERSTANDING THE STEPS

Within this book I discuss how to motivate yourself, research your possible careers, obtain a mentor, get an internship, create an effective résumé and cover letter, maximize your personal marketing efforts, and finally, how to interview. Why am I telling you how to accomplish these things? What do they have to do with finding a career? Read on to find out…

PREPARING YOURSELF TO PLAY BALL

Perhaps the most difficult task in this entire book is in *Step 1: Finding Your Fuel*. After all, say your Mom or guardian wants you to follow in their footsteps, but their career hold no interest for you. After much thought, you discover that your dream is to play pro baseball (imagine they have women's teams, too!). So you decide to make pro baseball your goal. Finding it within yourself to pursue your goal will take lots of courage and motivation. *Step 1—Finding Your Fuel* helps you understand goals and the different types of motivation it will take for you to achieve them. The courage is up to you!

Once you have wrestled with your goals and now have your direction, it's time to prepare yourself to enter the job market.

Instead of barging right into a business, it is best to first research the field to make certain it's a good fit for you. *Step 2—Recognizing Resources* lists some excellent places to read up on possible careers.

Once you decide to play professionally, you could read a book on the fundamentals of baseball. But when you go to a professional team and tell them you want to play ball and that you qualify because you read a book about it, they'll wonder what planet you came from. To get your dream job you will need workplace experience and a mentor.

School—especially college—is in many ways similar to reading a book and then trying to play ball with the pros. Imagine going up to a company and saying you want to manage a distribution center because when you were a sophomore you read a book on management and earned an "A" in the course and, therefore, you have the skill necessary to manage other people. Good luck, but most likely they'll boot you out of the office because they want real-life experience.

MENTORS AS COACHES

OK, so say you've read a book on baseball and you have the notion that you want to play professional ball. The logical next step you could take would be to find someone who already knows the intricacies of the game and can help put you on the right path.

In sports we call this person a coach. Every coach has a unique view of the game, tips for playing, and methods of motivation. No matter how different their perspectives are, based on their past experiences, all coaches have one goal in mind when they lead a team: Winning.

With this in mind, coaches are great assets and it is to your advantage to have a number of different coaches. Each one will add something unique to your game based on their talents and experiences. You can get the best results by obtaining several different coaches with diverse backgrounds and perspectives. Remember, even the best athletes in the world still have coaches.

In the world of work, we refer to coaches as mentors. Mentors are not here to be your training wheels on the bike of life; rather, they help you gain balance and direction until you can ride by yourself. As in baseball, it is best to have many different mentors with diverse backgrounds and viewpoints. This way you can take what you feel is the most beneficial to you and apply it not only to your job search but your philosophy of life as well.

Step 3—Make the Most of Mentors shows you how to search for and obtain mentors. This chapter, along with the rest of the book, should aid you in getting the mentors who would be most helpful to your life and your career.

Now that you have read the books and have a few coaches to assist you, what is next? Practice, of course.

INTERNSHIPS = PRACTICE

Once a coach helps you develop your motivation and inner drive, the next step is to get you onto the field. In other words, you might understand the game and be motivated to do well, but when you step up to the plate with no experience, you will realize that there is a lot more to the game than just studying about it. Practice not only hones your playing skills, it also improves your performance by giving you a feel for the game and its setting. It is one thing to hit a home run in practice; it is another to step up to the plate with a strong wind in your face, an ocean of freshly cut turf stretching to the horizon, and 20,000 irate fans yelling their opinions of you.

Practice in business is also essential. In business we call practice an internship. An internship allows you to experience the work environment you are interested in firsthand. Often the work is much different and less glamorous than what it looked like in the books, but the experience will give you direct exposure to a career you are considering. *Step 4—Internships: Learn to Earn* covers all the mechanics of internships. You will learn how to find an internship, how to obtain it, and how to maximize it. Internships give you valuable experience that makes you more marketable to potential employers.

RÉSUMÉS

Now that you have read the books, obtained the needed focus, and gained firsthand experience, how do you get on the team? Well you, or your agent, markets you to the team. Baseball players utilize statistics like errors, steals, home runs, and strikes to impress prospective teams.

In the job market, your achievements, experience, and recommendations are your statistics. All this information is contained in your résumé. Just as an agent gets a team interested in a player's future by showing them slides, statistics, and career highlights, your résumé is the marketing tool that summarizes your history and gives an idea of your potential.

Step 5—Personal Marketing: Selling Yourself gives you in-depth coverage and samples for preparing your resume and cover letter. It also includes often overlooked items such as thank you cards, phone messages, business cards, and fax cover sheets.

INTERVIEWS

If a team is particularly interested in a player, the team's management will invite the player to try out for the team. In the employment world, your tryout is the job interview. Interviews allow the prospective employer to take a closer look at applicants and evaluate their potential. *It is important to remember that it is not what you have done in the past that is most important, but what you can do in the future.*

Step 6—Interview Effectively shows you interviewing techniques that will help you successfully present yourself and your potential to a prospective employer. Take time to practice the sample questions for delivering a good interview.

Now that you have learned the fundamentals, gained insight from a coach, practiced on the playing field, talked with successful players, marketed yourself, and demonstrated your future potential—what do you do next? Take off your hat for the "Star Spangled Banner" and get ready to play ball!!

books ☞ *coach* ☞ *practice* ☞ *try out* ☞ *Major leagues!*

books ☞ *mentor* ☞ *internship* ☞ *interview* ☞ *Employment!*

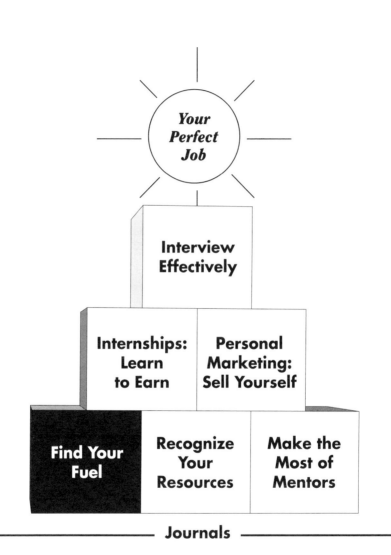

Your
Perfect
Job

Interview
Effectively

Internships:
Learn
to Earn

Personal
Marketing:
Sell Yourself

Find Your
Fuel

Recognize
Your
Resources

Make the
Most of
Mentors

Journals

Step 1
FINDING YOUR FUEL

Getting yourself motivated is the first critical step you must take to find your perfect job or internship—the rest *is* simply mechanics. Anyone can use the strategies in this book to assist them in their job search, but it is finding the motivation and desire within you that will make the difference in entering the job market. The key to finding a job is discovering and enhancing the belief within yourself that you are willing to put forth whatever effort is necessary to obtain the job of your choice. Once you make this decision, your perfect job is not far away.

IDENTIFYING YOUR CAREER: MONEY VS. HAPPINESS VS. UNEMPLOYMENT

There are two main types of motivation—mental and physical. Each of these motivates us to varying degrees; one extreme is positive and the other is negative. The strength of our motivation determines what we will or will not do, and what we can and cannot do. The goal of this book is to help you realize how to incorporate positive motivation into your life and create a plan to achieve your goals.

A mentor of mine told me that one of the greatest and most well-kept secrets in the industrialized world is "Everything you need you already have." Think about it. The only things you truly need to live are food, shelter, and clothing. You may or may not feel you have each of these needs fulfilled already, and if you don't, obtaining them should be your first priority. But, if most of our basic physical needs are already met, what motivates people to continue working so hard?

IDENTIFYING SHALLOW MOTIVATION

Rather than go into detail about the many types of shallow motivation, I will provide you with two examples:

EXAMPLE 1

Chris Jones lives in Big Town, Texas. He lives in a neighborhood where everyone knows each other. Chris feels that whenever one of his neighbors buys a new lawnmower or car he has to get one that is bigger and better. This is a futile effort to prove that he is "better" than they are. This senseless competition is repeated throughout the neighborhood with everyone trying to surpass their neighbors. Will Chris ever be satisfied with his "status" if he is always trying to be better than his neighbors? Probably not. Rather than finding happiness in what he has worked hard for, he feels compelled to surpass his neighbors. Will he find the happiness he wants by surpassing his neighbors? No. Someone will always come along with something bigger and better. Chris should evaluate his constant competition and look inside himself to see what is missing, rather than looking through his window at his neighbors.

If your goal is to accumulate material possessions, you will have trouble becoming truly happy because you will always want more "stuff." The most effective motivation is not based on money or "stuff." The following example illustrates one family's attempt to motivate their son:

EXAMPLE 2

The Thompsons, Bill's proud and well-meaning parents, used money to influence their son's actions. Throughout middle school, they offered Bill $10 for every "A" he earned on his report card. They hoped that this would entice Bill to do well in school. Does this teach Bill that education is valuable? That effort is rewarded? Or, does it merely emphasize that money is most important?

The problem with this type of motivation arose when the financial incentives were taken away. Once Bill turned sixteen and obtained his first job sacking groceries, the Thompsons decided that the $10 incentive was no longer needed. After all, Bill had a job and was making his own money. Do you think Bill continued to work hard in school without the monetary incentives? In some cases, yes; but in this case, no. The lesson learned was not that knowledge itself is more valuable than money, but that if you are not going to get paid for something, it is not worth the effort. The parents took an easier route than instilling positive motivation. Thus, their son Bill did not have a more powerful motivation within himself: *satisfaction in his accomplishments.*

Appreciating your own achievements is always much more rewarding.

Positive Motivation

Let's take a closer look at the difficult definition of positive motivation. Positive motivation—*inner satisfaction*—is more challenging to develop than shallow motivation. However, it is also the most effective method for pushing you to reach your goals—and the backbone of this book.

Focusing on Your Positive Side

Positive mental motivation springs from the desire that allows us to feel a sense of accomplishment, pride, and happiness with our work. An incident last year vividly portrays this:

A close friend of mine turned in a three-and-a-half page paper for a major grade in our literature class. This young man was extremely intelligent by any scale, but focused more on learning than on grades. The paper failed to meet the minimum four-page requirement set by the professor and my friend consequently received a "B+". Not a particularly disheartening grade, but the professor's comments accompanying the grade were startling.

"Tim," he said, "This is one of the most well-written, well thought-out magazines I have ever read. In my experience of writing for and editing national journals, I rarely have the opportunity to read such a fine paper. If you had written four pages, you would have definitely received an 'A.' "

Tim looked into the eyes of the accomplished professor and sincerely said, "Sir, not to offend you, but I felt my paper was complete at three-and-a-half pages. I did not want to diminish the quality of the paper by attempting to improvise another half page. I realize I did not meet your requirements, but in my mind this paper was finished where it ended."

The professor, shocked by these remarks, did not know what to say. Finally he told Tim to try and meet the requirements for his next assignment.

The point of this story is that Tim was not concerned with the grade, but with the quality of his work. Tim went on to earn one of only two "A's" given in the course for the semester. Moreover, he won the respect of the professor and his fellow students.

What separated Tim from other students, including me at the time, was that he possessed something much stronger than the satisfaction of receiving an "A." He was alive with *passion,* and it showed in everything he did.

It is often difficult to convince people that grades and evaluations are not everything and that inner happiness is most important. When they realize this, they truly find happiness within themselves. Not receiving an "A" in a class is not the end of the world, as long as you put forth your best effort. It is difficult, especially in our modern society of grades and competition, to find satisfaction in one's work regardless of the subjective value given. This applies to job satisfaction as well. Being happy at work is more important than making money.

HARNESSING POSITIVE MOTIVATION

One way a person can harness motivation in a positive way is through a "dream sheet." This is a collage of various things you desire. It can include words, pictures, and drawings. A dream sheet allows you to visualize your goals. In my room I have two dream sheets, one focuses on my family and the other focuses on places I would like to travel. The more specific your goals are the more likely it is you will achieve them. Remember to keep your goals in perspective, i.e., don't put your basic needs in jeopardy in order to purchase a fancy car.

I also like to carry a special object with me at all times, to remind me of my goals. I suggest that you find something that has to do with the *"why"* aspect of your job search. The object you carry could be a stone with *"Dream"* written on it, a bracelet from a vacation to Mexico, or a key chain with a picture of your family on it. Find something that motivates you and keep it close; it will remind you to stay focused on achieving the results you want.

EVALUATING YOUR GOALS

Sometimes what you think you want may not be what you need. For instance, a friend of mine retired from a successful medical practice at the age of forty. I spoke with him six months after he retired. He was not happy with his new life. He thought retirement would be great and stress-free, but having nothing to do was more stressful on him than when he practiced medicine.

You see, he had defined happiness as retiring. Once the act of retiring was achieved, what else was left? Life doesn't stop after you retire, but that was all he had planned. In time, he will probably adjust to the change, but will he ever gain the happiness and peace that he desires? It will be difficult for him unless he changes his perspective on happiness and begins to see life as more than a means to purchase material goods. He must find the inner desire, the passion, that will motivate him and provide him with the happiness he yearns for. In other words, he must find something within retirement that lights his fire and keeps him going.

No matter what, your life will be more meaningful and satisfying if you feel a sense of pride and accomplishment with your work. Developing this inner drive is essential to living life to its fullest, whether at work or at the beach.

It is the things in life you desire and the perspective you take that will determine your happiness and how much you will accomplish. *Viewing life as a challenge and a gift rather than a chore to be completed will enable you to find the satisfaction you seek.*

INCORPORATING YOUR HAPPINESS IN YOUR JOB HUNT

It is likely that you will be working for most of your life, so you should take more than your salary into consideration when deciding your future career direction. Ponder the old saying that "money is not everything" and think about all your options. Are you going to be happy and satisfied at your job a month, year, or five years from now?

Do you like the location? Is the traffic bearable? Do you like the weather (most people don't realize what a big change it is to move from one part of the country to another)? Do you like the company and the environment in which you will be working? Is the competition cutthroat, or do all employees work together to increase the shared pie? Is it a corporate ladder, where the person in front of you always makes more money than you? Is it an environment where they reward innovative ideas and performance, or reject change?

Evaluate the answers to these questions and determine if they fit within your goals and plan of attack. Otherwise, your performance may suffer and it will be a bad situation for everyone involved.

Be proactive about your job search. Research the industries you wish to work for thoroughly before you begin sending out résumés. Find out which companies have been downsizing and growing. What do the trade magazines say about the industry's future and who are the key players? When was the last time the company had layoffs, and was it industry-wide? What is the company's credit rating and what (if it's public) do investors think of it?

Things to always consider in a career are stress, average hours of work per week, vacations, whether business is seasonal, and what the industry is rapidly moving toward in the future. For instance, did you know that the U.S. is rapidly moving more toward being a service-oriented economy and less of a manufacturing economy? This does not imply that you should not pursue a career in manufacturing. Instead, it means that there are more aspects to consider in a potential career than just pay and status.

Finally, keep in mind all of the responsibilities and duties each career choice will demand of you. For example, there's no point in seeking a career as a veterinarian if you dislike animals, or in becoming a trapeze artist if you're afraid of heights.

Working Your Strategy

Focusing your plan of attack on your goals is the hardest part of the book, but once you have them aligned and begin to implement them in your daily activities and your job search your level of passion will continuously rise. For example, simply taking twenty minutes each day to write poetry (if one of your long-term goals is to be a poet) will enable you to find satisfaction every day with a small time commitment. Incorporate your long-term goals into your job search as best you can.

Avoiding Tunnel Vision and Focusing on the Big Picture

Now that you have determined your goals and are working your plan of attack, there is one hazard you should be aware of: tunnel vision.

One of my mentors, a successful businessman, told me a story to emphasize the importance of not getting "tunnel vision" when focusing on your strategies. He is about sixty-five years-old, has survived a quadruple bypass, and now lifts weights four times per week.

"Imagine you are at the bottom of a deep well. All around you is darkness, but looking up you can see a small circle of light. You are not quite sure what it is, but after much deliberation you decide that taking the chance to reach the light is better than staying where you are. So, you stick one foot into the wall on one side of the well and put the other foot on the other side. You brace one arm up against the side of the wall and then the other—now you are off the ground. Slowly you lift your foot up and plant it higher in the wall. Then you extend your arm and move your other foot. Inch by inch you progress toward that circle of light. Sometimes you grasp loose dirt and fall back, but eventually you catch yourself and begin moving upward again. Each step takes you closer to your goal and makes the circle of light brighter. Finally, after much struggling, you are just below the surface. You are tired and your body aches. This is the point where you are at the most risk, the point where you can fall the furthest. Slowly, you lift one hand up and grasp the outside of the well, lifting your arm after it. Then you do the same with your other hand. Now you slowly pull your body above the surface. Suddenly, you lift your head out of the well. *Wow!!* The world is suddenly all around you. It was there the whole time. No matter how low or high you were in the well, the world was always there. The only reason you did not know this was your perspective."

Life itself is a hard climb, sometimes a crawl, and loose dirt is often encountered. Focus on what you are working toward and you *will* achieve your goal. This book can guide you to the job you want, but keeping the bigger picture in mind is up to you.

No matter where you are in life, don't forget about the big picture. Don't let life pass you by because you are focused on the wrong priorities and limiting yourself from reaching your bigger goals.

BELIEVE IN YOURSELF

What you can achieve is only limited by what you think you can achieve. Believe in yourself and your abilities, realize the potential you possess, and nurture it to become the best you can be. Building this confidence takes time and dedication, but projecting this confidence is one of the most powerful tools you possess. Be proud of yourself, your achievements, and your goals. Always remember that no matter what your age or education, you have a marketable product in yourself. Use it. You can achieve anything you want once you decide to do it and take action!

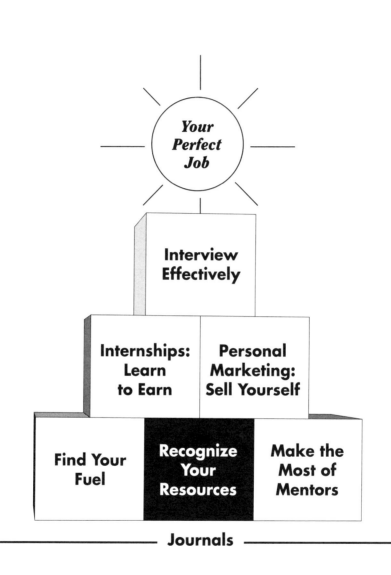

Step 2
RECOGNIZING YOUR RESOURCES

This chapter will show you where to find the information you need to make your job or internship search easier and more effective. The sources I recommend are found at most schools, colleges, libraries, bookstores, online, etc. They can usually be found at no cost. Keep in mind that a student's job search motto should be: *Spend your time—not your money*!

COLLEGE CAREER SERVICES OFFICE

The Career Services Office (CSO) is an invaluable asset to college students, regardless of academic major or career path. The job of the CSO is to prepare students to find jobs by connecting them with employers who are looking to fill positions. In other words, the CSO gives you a ready-made audience for your skills and education. It has contacts in almost all industries and career paths. In addition, the CSO staff has experience helping students like yourself and will provide valuable assistance in optimizing your job search.

However, all too often students fail to use the CSO to its full potential. Instead, they rely on themselves to make their contacts, or worse, do nothing at all. It is definitely possible to do everything yourself, but it is much easier to use the CSO. Make it a point to visit the CSO within the first week of classes and obtain a schedule of upcoming workshops and events. In this way, you can stay on top of your career opportunities.

Many CSOs also have some type of online database for storing your résumé that is easily accessible to recruiters. This database allows students to research companies and upcoming recruiting sessions. These systems usually allow you to "post" your résumé electronically. Therefore, if you meet the basic qualifications for an interview, you can automatically have your résumé sent to the recruiting team before they even arrive at your school!

The only way to learn if you meet the qualifications set by a company is by accessing the system and seeing what recruiting companies want. Basic qualifications for an interview often consist of classification, graduation date, experience, and grade point average.

If you cannot automatically "drop" your résumé to the recruiter because you do not meet the basic requirements, by all means obtain the recruiter's address or fax number and contact them directly to express your interests.

The CSO may not be able to allow you to schedule an interview. But if you speak with the recruiter and express your desire and enthusiasm to work for the company, they may be able to fit you into the schedule. Post your résumé on the database as early as possible since companies begin recruiting very early in the school year; update it as often as possible. In addition, place your e-mail address on any list server the Career Services Office promotes.

If your college has a CSO list server, you usually must send an e-mail to an address and tell them what you are interested in getting on the e-mail list. They will then add you to the list. Once you have placed your name on the list, you will receive updates regularly from the CSO regarding upcoming recruiters, events, and workshops that they are organizing. This is a valuable tool for staying aware of campus activity.

Now that you are signed up online, contact the CSO counselors. They can provide you with information on specific areas, such as a contact they may have and assist you by proofreading your cover letters. Tell them what careers you are interested in so they can help you as soon as possible.

Developing a relationship with the counselors can be a real asset, especially when companies arrive on short notice. If the counselors know what position you are interested in, they can contact you. Attend CSO events and become familiar with the counselors who work there. After all, you are paying for their services through your tuition so use them to their utmost benefit.

High School Counselors

Most high schools have some type of college counselor and/or a career counselor. In small schools, one person may fill both positions. It is important you familiarize yourself with your counselors and how they can help you. Regularly check with them about internships and other types of summer or part-time employment. If you are looking for a full-time job, the career counselor usually has an assortment of job opportunities she will gladly share with students. Use these resources—they are there to help you!

Libraries

Many universities and high schools have career libraries or online databases filled with a wide assortment of employment information. The librarian can help you find what you are looking for, just ask! It will help narrow your search if you include the industry, company, and career field you are interested in.

Libraries have information on everything from résumés to specific indus-tries as well as an excellent selection of *trade magazines*. These magazines are very important because they convey what the trends are within an indus-try and can provide names and addresses of key people to contact. I also look through the résumé postings from different schools across the nation. Many universities keep résumés on file from the top business schools across the nation. This shows you literally thousands of examples of how people compile their résumés. Look through these and find some styles you like, make a pho-tocopy of them, and use them as a template for your own résumé.

BOOKSTORES

If your school does not have some type of career library or career section, locate another one nearby and do research there. If this too is difficult, go to a book store, preferably a large one, and hang out for a few hours reading books in the career section. They should have plenty of books you can browse through that cover various types of career paths. Best of all, it's free!

BETTER BUSINESS BUREAU AND THE CHAMBER OF COMMERCE

I make it a point to contact the Better Business Bureau and Chamber of Commerce when researching jobs. They are an excellent source of current information on industries and specific companies in your area and can pro-vide you with numbers to contact other Bureau and Chamber chapters across the country. Give them a call.

PROFESSIONAL ASSOCIATIONS

Professional associations can provide tons of information on careers, indus-tries, and employers. They are my secret advantage for getting job leads. Their meetings are excellent places to gain firsthand knowledge from people who already have the career you are interested in. Do not be intimidated about attending the meetings; you are important enough to be there!

THE YELLOW PAGES

If you are having trouble locating a company in your industry, browse through the Yellow Pages and contact companies that look interesting. Then you can initiate an informational interview or request info on the company.

NEWSPAPERS AND MAGAZINES

Newspapers and magazines provide other inexpensive resources for career information. I recommend looking in large circulation business newspapers and magazines for articles about a specific industry or career path. There are several newspapers devoted entirely to the job search. Rather than subscribing to one of these, once again go to a bookstore or library and browse through them while enjoying a beverage. If you find something that grabs your attention, either write it down (cost-effective) or buy it.

JOB FAIRS

There are two ways to look at a job fair: as an excellent place to obtain free school supplies (mugs, cups, pens, highlighters, and more) or as a convention hall packed with a large number of potential employers just waiting for the opportunity to meet you. If you plan on taking the first approach, bring a backpack or something to fill with all of your free goodies. If you are after more than short-term gain, I recommend the second approach. View a career fair as one big job interview and be prepared to present yourself the best you can to get the job you want.

Prior to the career fair, the sponsoring organization usually distributes flyers listing what companies are scheduled to be in attendance and a map illustrating the layout. Review the list of companies for any that interest you. Once you have identified these, highlight them green, red, or yellow (any three colors will do), with green being the companies of highest priority, yellow important, and red being of the least interest.

If a company is of no interest to you, simply skip it and go on. Once you have finished highlighting each selection from highest priority to lowest, go back and rank all of the green companies sequentially, beginning with the one you want to see the most. Do the same for the yellow and then the red. What you have just done is prioritize the list of companies beginning with the ones of most interest to you, to the ones you are interested in but will not be upset about if you don't get to speak with their recruiters.

Now that you have identified and ranked the companies you would like to speak with, you need to formulate a *plan of attack* (see diagram on following page). Find each company's booth you're interested in on the convention hall map you are given. Highlight all of your green companies' tables green, and so on. As you are highlighting them, write your ranking number next to them. This will keep you focused and organized during the career fair.

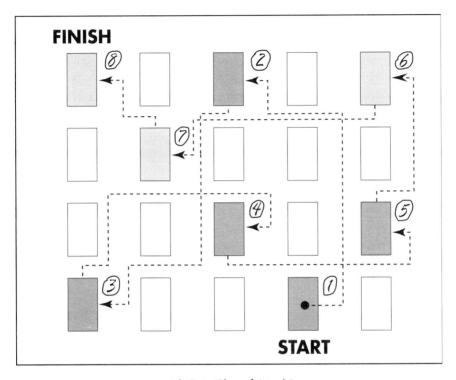

Job Fair "Plan of Attack"

Once you've got your plan of attack in shape, find a starting point and the easiest way to connect the numbers of the same color, trying to stay in a logical order (kind of like paint-by-numbers and connect-the-dots together). It is fine to skip around a bit if, say, a higher-number green booth is between two lower-number green booths. The key thing to do is stay within each color as best you can to visit with your priority companies first.

When at the career fair, see the companies in the order of the map you have drawn. Be sure you check off every booth you visit because you don't want to wait in line to speak to someone you have already spoken with. Plan on being able to talk with ten recruiters each hour. Some recruiters may just hand you a piece of paper saying where to send your résumé and cover letter, and take a copy for themselves. Other recruiters might be willing to talk with you and determine if they can assist you in any way. Realize that a recruiter at one of these career fairs may speak with over one hundred people in three hours, so don't be upset if they are not as friendly as you would like. They are there to share information and act as a "commercial" for their company. *Don't judge a company by a recruiter. That is equivalent to judging a book by its cover.*

I like to watch the recruiters in action at each booth and choose the one I think I can communicate with the best. It's definitely worth waiting a few extra minutes if you can finally speak with the recruiter who makes you feel most comfortable. I am not encouraging you to stereotype people, but if you feel more comfortable speaking with older recruiters, for example, then by all means wait to talk with older recruiters. If you feel more comfortable talking to women, then wait to talk to a woman. Anything you can do to feel more comfortable and professional will benefit the conversation you have.

JOB FAIR MANNERS

Now that you know what companies you want to see, it's time to decide what to bring and what to wear. I strongly encourage you to wear professional attire. Men should wear a suit, or at least a tie, dress pants, and a long sleeve shirt. Women should wear a business suit or some type of conservative outfit, preferably one with a tailored jacket. Keep all jewelry to a minimum.

If possible, obtain a name tag and attach it to the upper right side of your chest. You put it on the right side because most people shake hands with their right hand and this gives them the opportunity to read your name. Beside your first and last name, also put your graduation semester and year, your major (if you have one), and the college or school you are attending. Make sure the writing on your name tag is easily readable.

WHAT DO YOU BRING TO THE FAIR?

Step 6—Interview Effectively of this book should be read before you present yourself to recruiters. It contains helpful suggestions that will make the interviewing process go smoothly. *Step 6—Interview Effectively* discusses what you should wear, but what should you bring?

I discourage you from bringing a briefcase, solely because it looks a bit overwhelming. Unless you specifically need a briefcase to carry something that helps to market you better, do not bring one.

Instead, bring a portfolio binder. They usually have a large notepad, a place for pens, two card holders, and a place for your résumés. A portfolio binder is easy to carry around and you can get one for less than $10. I recommend spending a little bit more to buy something nicer if you can—remember, you are a professional now.

In the card holder fill one space with your own business cards (note: I provide sample business cards later in this book) and bring two nice pens that you know work. If you can, buy two nice metallic or wood-type pens. Once again, small touches like having nice pens display your professionalism.

Be sure there is plenty of paper in the portfolio binder. You might want to put in a fresh notepad. This pad comes in very handy. Before you arrive at the career fair, list the top ten companies you want to speak with and leave about five lines of space between each company name. This way, you will be prepared for the recruiters you want to meet most. As you finish with a recruiter, write down what you learned about the company or any steps for hiring that you should pursue. Basically, summarize their recommended action in your notepad.

On each business card you receive, write down a physical description of the person who gave it to you. This action is essential in order to help jog your memory if you happen to meet the recruiter again at a restaurant or conference room along with other recruiters. After a long day of speaking with thirty-plus recruiters, it becomes hard to remember what each one looks like, so you *need* to create a reminder. Now to the résumés.

JOB FAIR RÉSUMÉS

I always bring three different résumés to a career fair. In *Step 5—Personal Marketing: Selling Yourself*, I suggest personalizing each résumé for your desired employer. For job fair "interviews," you can write a different objective for each company you want to speak with, but I recommend just three.

The first one should be directed to the industry you are interested in, the second should address a specific segment or job in that industry, and the third should have a general objective about obtaining employment that maximizes your talents. Of course, you can bring as many résumés with specific objectives as you want, especially if you are interested in more than one industry. I separate the résumés in my holder by a sheet of brightly colored paper. This is an easy way to differentiate between the different objectives and allows you to find the résumé you are looking for quickly.

During the career fair you will be handed or offered a great deal of promotional information. Take whatever is offered—the more information you have the more you have to base your decisions on. If they insist you take some free "souvenir," oblige them. Many times recruiters try to get rid of as much stuff as they can so they do not have to bring it back to the office with them.

Besides offering your résumé, if you really like speaking to a certain recruiter, ask for a business card and the best way to contact them. When the recruiter hands you a card, hand her one of yours! It just might catch her off guard, and is another way to get your name into their hand.

Expanding on this idea, another way to gain more access to recruiters is by volunteering to assist in the career fair. This can be quite beneficial, if you still have enough time to sufficiently speak with all the recruiters in which you are interested. Some of my friends volunteered and were disappointed because they were so busy running errands that they did not have as much time to attend the career fair as they would have liked. However, others felt that they were able to talk with the recruiters on a more personal level and, as a result, gained an advantage.

A good thing to consider about volunteering is whether volunteers are given a thank-you party or special time to meet with recruiters. If a party is given, this creates a great opportunity to mingle with recruiters and should be taken advantage of, if possible.

After the fair send a thank you card or a letter to specific recruiters or companies that really appeal to you. Thank them for answering your questions and express your enthusiasm for working with them. Be sure to include your follow-up step, i.e., "I will call you on March 22nd, etc."

Thank you notes should be sent out the day that the event occurred. If you do forget to do this, and it is within three days, I suggest (but don't tell anyone I said this) that you backdate the cards. Sometimes, thank you cards just get lost in the mail for an extra day or three! Don't try and backdate a card too far because the cards are stamped the day they are mailed.

THE LAST RESORT

If you are really looking for any opportunity to make a contact, check out your local restaurants. Many times they keep business cards from local companies on their bulletin board. Often, you can find direct lines to people of varying industries and careers, while you are eating! Just be sure you don't take any cards out of the "win a free lunch jar."

THE INTERNET = WWW. YOUR NEXT JOB. NOW

The Internet is a priceless tool in your job search bag. I like to start with a search by industry using one of the popular search engines. Some industries even have a webpage through their professional association. Next, I search using the name of some of the companies I have either read about at the Career Library, in a trade magazine or online. Almost all companies have a website detailing their business products or services and their current employment opportunities.

Once you locate a company that interests you, either print their Web page as best you can or jot down a few sentences about them. Next, go to the Human Resources (HR) link or the hiring section. These links provide details to what the particular company is looking for and what each position requires. It also provides information on where to e-mail, mail or fax your résumé along with whom you can contact.

The other route to take is to search by occupation. Enter your desired occupation and go from there. Usually searching by occupation will uncover companies that either are focused on the occupation, employ the occupation, or are in some other way related to the occupation. Some companies even post "Job Search" databases for you to browse. This is an excellent way to learn about companies in the comfort of your home.

When you are online, you can visit my website at **www.jasondorsey.com**. It has lots of cool quotes, pictures, and free information.

NETWORKING

What exactly is *networking?*

Networking is truly an art form. It is finding connections with other people that might lead to something beneficial for you, or them. It is meeting people and helping them with something that they need or want. Networking is important when people have a common interest, say tennis. Sometimes networking is known as tracking down information through acquaintances.

Without a doubt, it is better to give than to receive in networking. The first rule of networking is to find ways you may be able to help someone and later find a way they may be able to help you. In other words, have a clear idea of what you want to get from a networking activity but intend to give rather than receive. Often, it is only when you give that people think enough about you to open a door for you in the future.

BEGIN AT THE BEGINNING

Networking for students starts in the same place as networking for business people. It can make all the difference when searching for an internship, mentor, or full-time employment. Believe it or not, you probably already know enough people to build a strong network—all you need to do is engage them.

When building your network, start with your family and close friends. Find out what occupation each person holds and how well you know them. Don't overlook any connection, no matter how small. For instance, on a tour of a university campus, my guide told me that the president of the university once personally took a prospective student on a guided tour of the campus. Wow, who might have such power? Not a millionaire's son (that probably would work, too), rather the student was the son of a man who often drove the president's limousine. Not a glamorous job, but the connection was solid and the university president was happy to help his loyal employee.

PLACES TO NETWORK

Draw a diagram of your existing family and friend networks as a visual resource. I recommend getting involved in a civic organization. There are many organizations targeted toward youth; while these are excellent, you should also try and gain entry to trade associations and adult civic organizations. These clubs often have restrictions by age and profession, but if you qualify, definitely get involved.

For instance, one of my friends is a member of a worldwide speaking organization. There are chapters of this organization oriented to college students, but he elected to join an adult chapter (18 and over) because he felt they would better improve his networking and professional speaking skills. If you really want to work on your networking skills, join a downtown chapter of an organization. These chapters usually include a wide variety of business people to meet, help and befriend.

Volunteering with a local charity organization of interest to you is also an excellent tool for networking. People from all backgrounds often come together to assist the less fortunate. Often the organizers of the events are well connected within the community and may be able to provide you with some assistance as long as you demonstrate your desire to work. Charity events such as banquets and dances are phenomenal places for networking. Unfortunately, the entrance fee is usually exorbitant because they are trying to raise money for a designated cause, so offer to volunteer!

Besides networking with friends and family, begin to network with other people in places that can assist you. As I said earlier in this step, a good place to begin is the career services office at your school or library. Add to this prospective employers. Stay in touch with a company regardless of advertised openings. This not only displays your enthusiasm to work for them, it also gives you a distinct advantage because most jobs are not advertised!

Following is an illustration of how an internship network might develop:

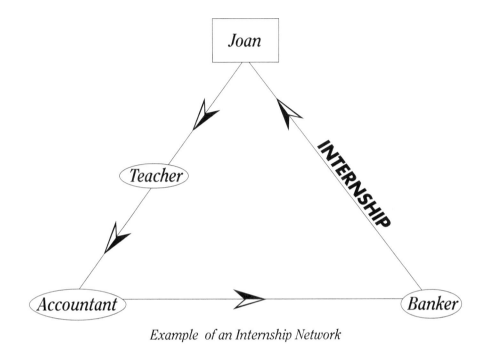

Example of an Internship Network

NETWORKING "NO-NO'S"

People often allow their friends or other contacts to use their names as a method of referral or introduction. This is an excellent way to meet people, but there are two key things to consider: Does the person whose name you are using reflect you in a professional way? By the same token, will the person whom you allow to use your name represent you in a positive way? If the person is not always courteous and professional, do not allow them to use you as a reference. You must also pay attention to treating your reference names with care. Remember, an old saying states that the best judges of a person's character are the people with whom he surrounds himself.

Importantly, avoid dropping names! It's great that you know the CEO of so-and-so company, but why are you telling me? If it isn't information that will help them, then often people feel you are bragging and immediately brand you as such. Being branded a name-dropper can really put a dent in your networking effectiveness.

STAY ORGANIZED

Whatever networking strategy you use, it is important to keep your progress organized through a database or some type of filing system. This simplifies things when someone whose name you do not recognize leaves a message for you asking to call her back right away because they may have a job opening. If you are well organized, you can find her name and determine who she is and what company she represents. A day planner or other organizer is a must for your networking and job search activities. These often have places to put your business cards as well as those you collect from others. There should be a calendar, address, and phone number section. Always keep your day planner with you while you are trying to find a job!

Start networking with prospective employers eight months before they begin hiring. Most full-time hiring is completed for college students well before May of their graduating year. By waiting until after winter vacation to begin the job search, many students miss out on valuable time they have during winter break as well as the opportunity to get to know the recruiters before most people do. *Remember, any advantage you can create for yourself boosts your odds of a successful job search.* Now that you have compiled a long list of names, addresses, phone numbers, companies, etc., what is next? The informational interview.

THE OFTEN UNDER-APPRECIATED INFORMATIONAL INTERVIEW

The informational interview is different from the employment interview discussed in Step 6, because you are not seeking a job and you are the interviewer rather than the interviewee.

What you do is request to speak with someone from a particular career field of interest to you in order to gain information. These meetings are usually short and somewhat informal. Always dress professionally (as detailed in *Step 6— Effective Interviewing*), bring numerous questions, and review the pre-interview checklist (also detailed in *Step 6*). Your research on the industry to be discussed will be very important during the interview.

Keep in mind that you are not interviewing for a job so do *not* ask for one. You will quickly lose the trust you have built during the conversation by asking for a job. Sometimes a job or internship offer is extended as a result of the informational interview, but leave it to the person you are interviewing to make that decision.

STEP 2 SUMMARY

Remember, there are career resource opportunities all around you. Keep your eyes, ears, and mind open and I know you will be successful! If you get stuck, ask for help.

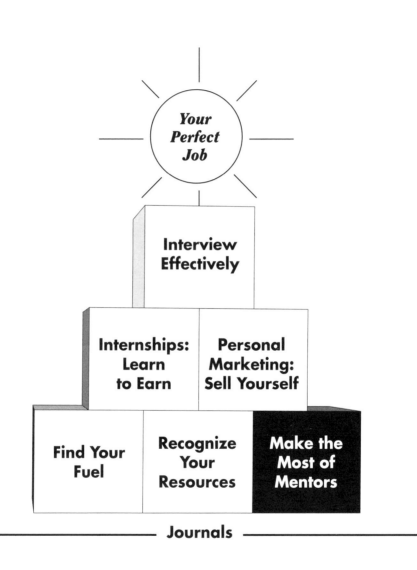

Your Perfect Job

Interview Effectively

Internships: Learn to Earn

Personal Marketing: Sell Yourself

Find Your Fuel

Recognize Your Resources

Make the Most of Mentors

Journals

Step 3
MAKE THE MOST OF MENTORS

If anyone has made the most significant difference in my life, it has been my mentors. Consistently, their encouragement, guidance and wisdom have kept me on the path to achieving my career and personal goals.

A mentor is a *trusted counselor* or *guide*. Mentors are probably the least valued yet most helpful asset a student can have when entering the job market. As outlined in *Preparation: Finding Your Focus*, a mentor is like a baseball coach, each with a unique outlook on the way to play the career game. Regardless of your age or perceived abilities, a mentor can benefit you.

Mentors not only provide you with massive amounts of insight that they have accumulated from experience, they also provide an excellent place to build your networking contacts. They may not specialize in your area of interest, but once you gain their confidence, they might introduce you to someone who is in your prospective field.

I recommend obtaining two to three mentors who vary in age, background, profession, and gender. One of my mentors retired at the age of thirty, another is in his mid-sixties and lifts weights four days a week. Each one has offered me different insights into what is valuable, both in life and in the employment world.

Finding a mentor is similar to looking for a job that you would really like—it takes time, persistence, patience, and acting on opportunities.

If you currently do not have a mentor, you can begin by finding one in the field you want to pursue, such as entrepreneurship, marketing, manufacturing, modeling, medicine, etc.

A good place to look for mentors is in the media. Don't be intimidated by a person's title or status: they are all human beings, no matter how invincible they may appear. If you feel a person can help you, get in touch with her and tell her that.

If contacting a company CEO sounds too intimidating, try reaching a vice president or manager. These people are still quite influential, but they also may have more time to devote to you. I recommend contacting people halfway up the corporate ladder, as they are probably younger than upper management and also more flattered by your request.

Remember, even if someone does not have a fancy corporate title they still may have a lot of information to offer. Consider asking community leaders, religious leaders, and people with an unprecedented drive to succeed to become a mentor to you. These people make excellent role models as well as mentors and friends.

FINDING YOUR ELUSIVE MENTOR

Is the person you want to contact high up the ladder in a corporation? Then a good place to begin is by contacting the local branch office and asking for an address where the person may be contacted. Don't initiate contact with a prospective mentor via the phone; often they are busy and won't answer messages from people they do not know. If the branch office does not have the executive's address, ask for a phone number where you can contact the main corporate office. Once given, call this office and ask for the address where you can reach the potential mentor. Also, obtain the correct spelling of your potential mentor's name; misspellings display a lack of professionalism. If at all possible, obtain the person's box number or mail stop as this helps expedite the mailing process. Be sure to address the envelope directly to whom you want to contact.

If you read about a prospective mentor in some type of magazine or newspaper, and the article does not contain the person's employer or any other traceable details, contact the publisher and have them transfer you to the article's writer. Most people, regardless of their desire for seclusion, have a mailing address accessible to the public. If this is not the case, inquire into an e-mail address or other means of contact, such as a fax number.

If a person's employer is mentioned, such as partner at the law firm of Kudos, Kudos, and Kudos, look through the phone book or call local information (1-411) to locate a means of contacting the person. If the contact lives in an area far from you, call local information and obtain the area code for the person's business and then call long-distance information (area code) 555-1212. Remember, there is a charge each time you call local or long-distance information from your home. If you need two or more numbers, ask the operator to give you as many numbers as possible verbally and then play the recorded number for the other company. This saves you the cost of another call, which can add up if you are contacting many people. All of these phone numbers can also be found on the Internet!

Sometimes professional search services, such as doctor or lawyer referral companies, can help. They do not charge the person calling, rather the referred physicians, so you incur no initial expense (it's calculated into your bill if you use their services). Referral services can be particularly helpful if you are attempting to contact a specific field within a general career path, such as anesthesiology in the medical field.

If you really want to cut costs or are having trouble obtaining a central number for a large company with dozens of branches, call toll-free information at (800) 555-1212. Companies, especially large ones, often make their main lines toll-free to better serve customers. Ask the operator for the main line or the number to their central office.

MONITORING PROGRAMS

Many universities, high schools, communities, civic organizations, and corporations have some type of mentor program or executive shadowing program in place to help students obtain a mentor. These programs are selective, but if you follow my guidelines for applications and interviews found in *Steps 5 and 6*, your chances of obtaining a mentor through one of these programs will be greatly increased.

CONTACTING YOUR MENTOR

Now that you have the name, address, phone number, or e-mail address for a prospective mentor, role model, or contact, what is the next step? Write them of course!

In the first letter, the key is to convey your enthusiasm and desire to meet with them. These people are quite busy so your best bet is to be sincere and brief. Explain why you selected them and how they can help you. You can even refer to the article you saw them in. Keep the letter short and to the point.

I like to begin by introducing myself and relaying some fact, such as that I attend a certain college, or that I am 18 years-old. Keep the introduction brief, but convey enough information so that they know you are someone who would make the most of their time. *Money you can recover; time you can't.* A good idea is to end the first paragraph by asking them to be your mentor.

The second paragraph should explain why you chose them. Tell them what you think you might like to do with your life and how you think they can help you to get there.

The closing paragraph should thank the person in advance for his or her time. Make certain that your letter flows well. You want to succinctly convey the literate, intelligent, motivated person you are.

Oftentimes, important people have many "gatekeepers" or people who decide what messages, letters, and other means of contact their employer receives. Usually these are secretaries or assistants who sort through everything and decide which items warrant attention. Persistence and determination make the difference as to whose letters are answered, so do not be afraid to write them once per week. It may be a cliché, but the squeaky wheel gets the grease.

If you are young, your age alone can be a big selling point; that's why I encourage you to start "recruiting" mentors as early as possible. This helps you because the older you get, the more achievements you have, and the better connected you become.

Mentor Mindset

Asking someone to become your mentor not only conveys your trust in them, it also demands a great deal of responsibility (if correctly positioned), and is a big honor. I try to meet with my mentors (I have four) every two weeks. Asking someone to be your mentor is like asking a parent to help you make the most of your life—they are there to support you and help you to learn from their mistakes as well as their triumphs.

They may suggest a restaurant, book, course of study, or missing a class to enjoy a beautiful day (I don't advocate this, but I do see the underlying implications). Mentors don't provide you with training wheels for a bike ride so much as they help to give you the initial balance, support, and vision you need to pick your own path and ride by yourself.

Meeting with Your Mentor

When planning to meet with your mentor, select a place that is convenient for both of you. If you need to, find a place more convenient for them since they are the ones making time for you in their schedule. I generally allot between 35 and 45 minutes, but give yourself an extra 15 to 30 minutes in case the meeting is going well and runs over. If your mentor is not on a busy schedule that day and the conversation is going well, it is fine to stay longer than the designated time; just make sure it is convenient for him/her.

Things to consider when selecting a location are how noisy and smoky it is. Is there available parking, and how do you get there (will you or your mentor need directions)? Would a person coming there for lunch in a business suit feel uncomfortable? If the place is too noisy, you will have to shout at each other and little will be accomplished. A smoke-filled room may cause one or both of you to experience allergies. (Always assume the person does not want a smoky environment unless he/she specifically asks for it). If the prospective mentor feels out of place, he/she will be focused more on the setting and how uncomfortable it is rather than the conversation.

Do not be disheartened if a potential mentor can't meet with you immediately. Professionals are quite busy and often have their schedules planned ahead of time. Understand their situation and be happy they are taking time to speak with you. Lunch might be their only break in a stressful day and thus might not the best time to meet with you. A late afternoon meeting at a restaurant or coffeehouse could be ideal. Make sure you call a day ahead of time to reconfirm the appointment time and place. While it's great to see your mentor as much as possible, avoid dropping by unannounced.

MECHANICS OF THE MEETING

Before meeting with your mentor, prepare an agenda. Always prepare more topics than you think you will need. The meeting will go by quickly, so do not try to cover everything in one session. Remember, you asked for their assistance, so let them help you.

Be sure to arrive at least fifteen minutes before the meeting is scheduled to begin. This will give you time to survey the meeting place and prepare yourself physically and mentally.

Check the *My Perfect Job*™ Pre-Meeting Checklist included in *Step 6 —Effective Interviewing* before the meeting. Little things like food in your teeth, dirty fingernails, or bad breath can really hurt the outcome of the meeting. If you are prone to sweaty hands keep a tissue in each of your pockets in case you get nervous. Also, if you have one, turn off your cellular phone. These things are annoying during a meeting and can negatively affect your prospective mentor's assessment of you.

Be sure not to lie or exaggerate when talking with your mentor. It is one thing to keep your guard up if you are uncertain about the mentor (that is the purpose of the initial meeting). It is another to lie in order to impress him. Do your best not to dominate the conversation. You already know everything you are going to say, and if you are talking you are not listening.

Avoid getting too personal, too fast. The initial meeting is a chance to feel one another out, and talk about your life and career goals. They might even connect you with someone else who could help. Also, have answers to the questions: "How can I help you?" and "Why did you select me?"

I suggest you bring a pen, paper, a day planner, and a few dollars to buy a drink or other incidentals. Write down only what you absolutely must. While they may find it flattering at first that you are writing down every word they say, this quickly wears off and takes away from the conversation, making it seem more like an interrogation.

A personal note: If the person you are meeting with uses explicit language while talking, this is ironically a good sign because it shows that they are comfortable with you. No matter how relaxed they become with the conversation, be sure not to lose your professionalism. You don't have to use the same language in return.

End the meeting on a positive note if possible. Even if you can't remember all the tips here, just remember to be yourself!

FOLLOW-UP

Be sure to send a thank you card the same day of the meeting. Phone or write to update your mentor periodically, say once per month. Let them know how you are doing and how you are progressing with whatever tips they gave you during your last meeting. Keeping in touch is crucial to building a strong relationship. Taking action on their suggestions shows you value their opinions

Mentors can provide a critical launching pad for *Step 4: Interning: Learn to Earn.*

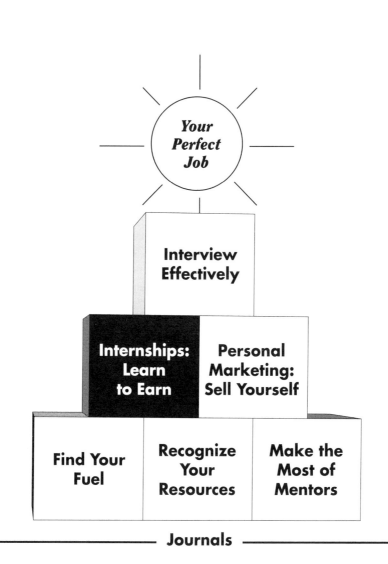

Your Perfect Job

Interview Effectively

Internships: Learn to Earn

Personal Marketing: Sell Yourself

Find Your Fuel

Recognize Your Resources

Make the Most of Mentors

Journals

Step 4
Internships: Learn to Earn

Along with your firsthand insight to a possible career path, one of the best tools for enhancing your job search marketability is an *internship*. Any internship you can obtain is great, especially if you receive payment for it. But, if you are undecided about a potential career path, and especially if you are young, I recommend the three-hour-per-week free internship. No paycheck? Read on and see why...

Finding an Internship

Select a career path, industry, or corporation that you are interested in. Find the office of a company within this field that employs your position of interest and is conveniently located to where you live. Walk in with enthusiasm, a résumé, and wearing business attire. Ask the receptionist if you can speak with someone in the department you're interested in, and then tell that person that you would like to work for free! No paycheck?! Not in the immediate future, but this internship can pay off big for you in the long run.

For example, the summer before I began college I wanted to work in the securities industry, but I had no background or contacts. I went down the phone book, calling brokerage houses to see if any had summer internship positions available. Finally, I found one and scheduled a 30-minute appointment with the branch manager.

Basically, I walked in, presented my résumé and a quick background of myself and my interests, and then told him that I wanted to work for free a few hours or days per week! He liked my enthusiasm and willingness to work for free to gain firsthand understanding of the industry and to see if it was something I wanted to pursue further. This approach worked so well that I was immediately hired and I started the following week!

Optimizing Your Internship

Often, internship work may be unglamorous. Still, you learn the most about an industry not from the work you do, but from the people you work alongside.

Instead of thinking about all the money you could be making at a paying job, focus on the information and connections you are gathering. These are definitely worth much more than being paid $6 per hour.

For instance, I did research for a broker on blue chip stocks. We often would go out to lunch and talk for an hour about the industry. In the three weeks I spent researching the stocks and talking to him, I believe I learned more than I would have had I been enrolled in a finance course for a year.

Take as much material home as allowed, and do not be shy about asking questions or gaining recommendations on books, magazines, or other resources they think might help. However, be sure to differentiate confidential material from public material and do not pass sensitive information to people outside the company. Definitely attend all employee events you are invited to and display your enthusiasm. These events are great networking opportunities.

Many times, promotional material, especially industry-produced, neglects to highlight the unglamorous aspects of a career. While interning, speak with a variety of people from different positions and compile their opinions on the industry and its future. Now you know the inside story!

Interning can be compared to learning a foreign language in the country where it is spoken compared to studying it in a classroom. This immersion technique really works. It's like attending an informational interview three days a week.

Interact with employees as much as possible. Eating with them, even the big bosses, is an excellent opportunity to learn firsthand about the business. If you are offered this opportunity, seize it. You have already shown your dedication by working for free.

I also suggest you spend some extra time networking with recently recruited people about the company's recruiting process and how they got their job. They may provide you with some insight into the job search process as well as specific information when dealing with a potential employer.

Every time someone recommends a book or trade magazine or gives you tips, write it down in your journal (at the end of this book). Use your journal to its fullest extent by recording your day-to-day activities as well as your thoughts and any other important information you collect.

Leaving an Internship

Unfortunately, not all internships are created equal. If after three weeks you do not like the internship, thank them for the opportunity and submit your resignation. It is wise to give at least one week advance notice so that the company is not caught off-guard. No matter how much you dislike the internship and/or the people you work with, leave on a positive note. In the future you might need them as a reference.

CONTINUING THE INTERNSHIP

On the other hand, if you enjoy the internship, you may volunteer to work more hours. Don't ask for money even after you have worked there for some time. You probably were not the type of person (either because of age or experience) that they would normally hire, and you might lose credibility with the management if they think you were just trying to get a job through the back door. However, it is a different situation if you initially state that you want to intern for three weeks and that, if they like your work, you will negotiate a salary. If you are still undecided about which career path to choose, I recommend interning at two companies, in two different fields, for two hours per week. The time commitment is minimal and the hands-on experience can help you make your decision.

GETTING A RECOMMENDATION

Look at your internship as a huge vault full of knowledge waiting for you to open it and begin learning. If you are in good standing at the end of the internship, inform your boss and advise other people you work with that you would appreciate (not demand) a written letter of recommendation.

Don't be intimidated by someone's title when asking them for a recommendation. Your enthusiasm, work ethic, and free assistance should be more than enough reason for them to happily comply.

I prefer to ask for a generic recommendation phrased "To Whom It May Concern," which includes some specific details from their experience with you that could prove helpful to a recruiter assessing your potential value to a company. The reason I suggest having your coworkers or boss draft one generic letter is that it saves you the time and hassle of calling them once a week and asking them to change the heading so that you can send another copy of it. They may even offer to make five to ten copies of the recommendation and sign them all. As soon as you get these letters of recommendation, file them carefully so they will be safe and you can easily access them.

Should your potential employers wish to contact your references personally, have them call the numbers provided on your letters of recommendation.

If you still feel uncomfortable asking for recommendations, do not stress over it. The knowledge you have gained probably outweighs what the recommendation could have done for you. Even if you are able to work only one hour per week, you still have *experience*, and that is just another way to separate you from the rest of the job seekers.

THE PAID INTERNSHIP

Once you have experience, you can obtain either another internship (for pay) or begin looking for a full-time job. Usually, interns who work for free are young people like you who would likely have met great resistance obtaining a job using any other method. However, completing a free internship gives you valuable experience that makes you more marketable!

SHADOW FOR A DAY

If you still feel that interning requires too much time, I suggest shadowing someone in your potential career for a day. Shadowing involves following someone around for a specified period of time to discover what it is they do during a typical day. All you have to do is call or write and make your request. The worst they can say is no, and at that point you are still ahead of the position where you started. Keep contacting people and you will definitely create a job-shadowing opportunity for yourself.

FOLLOWING UP

Remember to end your internship or shadowing experience on a positive note. Thank your boss, coworkers, or the person you shadowed in a follow-up letter. Tell them what you learned and how happy you were to be a part of their organization. As always, keep in touch with them from time to time and let them know how and what you are doing.

In *Step 5—Personal Marketing: Sell Yourself*, you will find several examples of thank you notes which can help you write your own. You will also discover how to use your internship experience to strengthen your résumé!

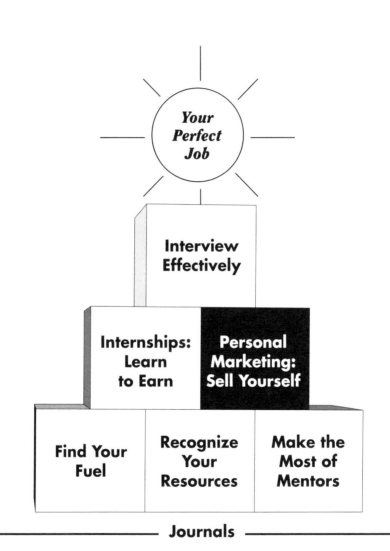

Your
Perfect
Job

Interview
Effectively

Internships:
Learn
to Earn

Personal
Marketing:
Sell Yourself

Find Your
Fuel

Recognize
Your
Resources

Make the
Most of
Mentors

Journals

Step 5
PERSONAL MARKETING:
SELLING YOURSELF

Once you have set your goals, identified potential career paths, formulated a plan of action, obtained an internship and mentors, it's time to start marketing yourself!

What is the difference between marketing yourself and someone trying to sell you a new kind of car? Not much, believe it or not. As a car company attempts to persuade you with reliability, performance, and price through various media (TV, radio, print), you will wage your own advertising campaign targeting employers. In other words, you will advertise your skills and potential with your marketing tools (résumés, business cards, phone calls, etc.) and thus highlight all the reasons they will want to hire you. It is important to make a good impression at each opportunity.

COMPLETING THE JOB APPLICATION

The application is an often overlooked marketing tool. Impressions are extremely important when completing an application, especially if it is the first contact you have with the company and are not submitting a résumé. Recruiters have nothing else to go by at this point, so do what you can to separate yourself from the rest of the applicant pool.

When completing an application, *type it* if at all possible! Typing the application once again demonstrates how serious you are about the job and that you are willing to put in extra effort to gain greater benefits. If you have poor handwriting, you should definitely type the application.

If you do not have access to a typewriter or a computer, it's not the end of the world. Just make sure you *neatly* print the information the application asks for in blue or black ink only. Many times the hiring department receives dozens, often hundreds, of applications for any one position. They are not going to take the time to decipher poor handwriting. If the application is illegible or even hard to read, it will find itself in the trash along with any chance you had of getting the job. The first impression they see is the neatness and completeness of the application. Sloppiness hurts your chances, so take your time and do it right. Your excellent interpersonal communication skills and winning personality will not save you if the potential employer does not want to interview you because your application looks bad.

Sometimes, the application will be a simple double-sided black-and-white copy, especially for summer jobs. If this is the case, by all means make a few copies and practice. This way, you will have a few copies if you mess up.

The first thing employers usually look for on an application is work experience, closely followed by education, accomplishments, and references. Depending on the position, they may also look at desired pay. I recommend asking for more money than you think they will pay, but stay realistic. Express to them that you are worth paying a little extra to have on their team.

When deciding whom to use as references, avoid young people and people who may not convey the impression you want. Be aware that people often judge you by your peers, so select those who will convey a positive image of you. Friends are alright as a last resort, but avoid using family members, especially if they have the same last name as you—unless they are famous!

I strongly recommend that you submit professional connections as references. If you have none, teachers or community leaders are fine, and don't forget your religious leader. Basically, anyone who displays the leadership and commitment to success that you want to portray, and who knows you personally, can be a valuable reference. Make certain the people you submit as references know that you are using them in this capacity. Especially in large corporations, it is hard to remember every person who has worked there, so make sure they know your plans before you use their names. It doesn't look good if your reference does not remember you.

Companies often check backgrounds and references, so definitely *do not lie or omit requested information*. It will result in either you not getting hired or your termination when they discover your deception. In some cases, the employer has the opportunity to pursue criminal action if you lied on your application. This is particularly true of federal jobs. It's one thing to say you worked from April through June when you worked from April *20* through June *5*. It is quite another thing to create a fake company and say you worked there.

List any awards you have won that are related to the job as well as any unusual experiences or expertise. Be sure to indicate any skills you have such as CPR certification or foreign language proficiency. Anything you can do to positively separate yourself from the other applicants is a must.

Proofread the application at least twice, once from front to back and then from back to front. It sounds like a lot of work for an application, but putting your phone number in place of your social security number does not make a good impression.

If you are asked to complete an application right before your interview, have at least three references handy, including names, addresses, titles, phone numbers, e-mail addresses, and your relationship to each reference. It does not look professional to ask the secretary for a phone book or to take the application home because you forgot your day planner. As the Boy Scouts say, *"Be prepared."*

SUBMITTING THE APPLICATION

The impression you leave when picking up and dropping off the application should not be overlooked. Dress well and be polite to *all* the employees you encounter, regardless of their perceived importance. Being rude to someone because you think they are unimportant will keep you unemployed. They already have a job with the company, so be respectful!

For instance, I once worked at a business where the manager would ask if anyone had picked up applications. If someone had, he would ask our impression of them. Leaving a bad impression can definitely hurt your chances of obtaining a job. Also, keep in mind that receptionists sometimes chat with their bosses. If they get a bad feeling about you, they will convey this.

Even the lowest people on the totem pole can greatly influence your prospects of getting hired. A friend told me that he was working at a restaurant when, one day, an applicant was standing outside the restaurant shouting rude comments about the interviewer into a cellular phone. A few minutes later a busboy who had seen the same event told the manager about it. The manager took the application and threw it in the trash. He thanked the busboy, because he had planned to make the applicant an offer the next day. It's always good to avoid hiring a bad employee.

THE COVER LETTER

Even if you must complete an application for a position, for professional jobs it will most likely accompany a cover letter and a résumé.

The cover letter is a necessity if you want to have your résumé read. The goal of the cover letter is to make the reader want to look at your résumé. If you submit a poorly constructed cover letter, the recruiter may not even glance at your résumé or application.

No matter how well you know the person who will be receiving your résumé, never send one without some type of cover letter. Keep the cover letter short and to the point. The letter's length should be no more than three paragraphs at the most. Recruiters spend less than 30 seconds reading your résumé, so how much time do you think they will spend on a letter introducing yourself? Probably less than they do on the résumé. The key to making a cover letter effective is to make its contents important and brief.

Convey your enthusiasm in your cover letter. The basic format is to introduce yourself, state the reason why you are writing (applying for the position), and how you learned about the position *(Beginning)*. Display some of your knowledge of the company or industry and why you are qualified or different *(Middle)*. Your next intended step is followed by a conservative and positive closing *(End)*. This format is very basic and can be altered depending on the audience and your intention.

Avoid exclamation marks but do express your interest in the company and your motives for this interest. Be sure to include your name and address at the top and use a professional format (see examples) and list all ways of contacting you (e-mail, etc.). If responding to an advertisement, mention where you saw the ad but avoid talking about how much you like that particular paper. Make the recruiter want to look at your résumé, not the newspaper that ran the advertisement.

When writing a cover letter on a computer, use features such as spelling and grammar checks and always have someone proofread the letter. Having someone else proofread your work is very important. When we proof our own material, we sometimes memorize it rather than read it and this leads to undetected errors.

To speed up the process, send the letter and résumé directly to a specific person in the company's Human Resources (HR) department. Even if you have to call and find out the recruiter for your region, do so because it helps to convey your professionalism. At all costs avoid putting "To Whom It May Concern" on the cover letter. The more specific the better.

If you know the person to whom you are sending the letter, remind them of how you met in the first paragraph. It is important to keep in mind that recruiters attend numerous career fairs each month and receive dozens of phone calls every day. Be as specific as possible about your initial or last method of contact. Also, if you have a mutual friend who networked you to the addressee of the letter, be sure to state this in the first paragraph. Sign your name, but avoid flashy signatures!

CHANGE THE NAMES

Some people use a generic cover letter and simply change the names. This is fine as along as you remember to change *all* of the names. Too often, people write great generic cover letters but forget to change all the names. In effect, they are telling the recruiter they look forward to working at another company!

QUICK TIP

An easy trick I discovered when sending a cover letter in a #10 envelope is to fold the enclosures in such a way that it looks professionally done. The way you do this is: fold your cover letter in thirds, as small as possible. Next, place the folded cover letter beside your résumé and fold the résumé until it is about a quarter of an inch larger than the cover letter when folded. Make sure the cover letter fits inside the résumé and that the résumé fits inside the envelope with the front flaps overlapping.

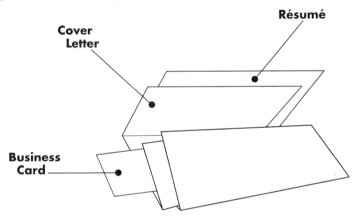

People too often believe that the résumé is the first impression recruiters have of you, when actually this is given by the cover letter. Make it a standing ovation!

CERTIFIABLY ON-TIME

I send almost all of my correspondence, excluding thank you cards, via certified mail, and recommend you do so if you can afford the cost. This service is excellent because you know what day your mail was received and you learn the name of the person who signed the return card. Occasionally, a letter you mail may get lost in an HR department, so keeping the return card will help the department "find" your correspondence. This also makes it easier to follow-up later, because you can tell the recruiter *exactly* what day your letter was received and *by whom*.

SAMPLE COVER LETTER #1

Rebecca Garcia
9173 Helons St.
Boston, Wisconsin 62843
(312) 555-3645
rcgarcia@collegemail.edu

December 2, 1996

Michelle Jamison
Employment Coordinator
Big Boat Company
7 New York Plaza
New York, New York 11924

Dear Ms. Jamison:

    We spoke on November 27, 1996 regarding my desire to intern with the hospitalities division of Big Boat during the summer of 1997. At your request, enclosed is my résumé and one letter of recommendation. I have experience working in the hospitalities field at a local hotel and would like to broaden my experience through summer employment on your cruise ship. Many aspects of the hospitalities field hold my fascination, including entertainment, customer service, and food preparation. Spending a summer away from home will not be a conflict, as I look forward to new challenges and experiences.

    Please contact me if I can provide further information or references that will facilitate the application process. If an on-site interview is necessary, the best time for me is during my Winter Vacation which runs from December 20, 1996 through January 10, 1997. Thank you for your assistance; I will contact your office on December 15.

Sincerely yours,

Rebecca Garcia

Encl: résumé/b-card/recommendation

SAMPLE COVER LETTER #2

Anthony Turner
7142 Ellis St.
Arlington, Texas 71208
(817) 555-9164

November 5, 1996

Gary D. Finley
Director - Commercial Human Resource
The Computer Partners, Inc.
Post Office Box 63422
Dallas, Texas 75266-3422

Dear Mr. Finley:

I am submitting my résumé in response to your advertisement in the *Local Newspaper* for a computer programmer. I have three years computer programming experience and a degree in computer science from Technical University. Currently, I manage a small computer store but am looking for new and exciting challenges. The job opportunity at The Computer Partners, Inc. contains the work flexibility and creativity I am seeking.

Significant Achievements include:

• Managed four full-time employees
• Supervised cash flow for business with $150,000 annual revenue
• Understanding of latest software, including Delta PHBS
• Fluency in Spanish as well as English
• B.S. in Computer Science from Technical University

The position with The Computer Partners, Inc. is exactly the employment position I desire. I am excited about the potential fit between us and would like to speak with you further regarding your employment openings. I will contact your office on March 7 to follow up on my application status. Thank you for your assistance.

Sincerely yours,

Anthony Turner

A RÉSUMÉ: YOUR PERSONAL BILLBOARD

Your résumé is your strongest marketing tool outside of an interview—think of it as your *personal billboard*. On the average, you have approximately seven seconds to look at a billboard before you pass it on the road. That's not much time, but somehow the message *is* communicated. Most recruiters spend only fifteen to thirty seconds looking at your résumé. Therefore, the key is to have the message you want to communicate as precisely focused toward your audience as possible.

Billboards highlight, bolden, or illuminate key parts of their messages and you should as well. Unfortunately, colored résumés and illustrations don't get the response that a colored or illustrated billboard does, but you can still borrow the techniques. In your résumé, use underlining, capitalization, bolding, and different fonts and sizes to draw the recruiter's attention to the information you think is your best selling point.

THE OBJECTIVE OF THE RÉSUMÉ

Besides your experience and education, the first thing your hiring audience is going to look for on your "billboard" is your objective. The way you focus your "billboard" to your audience is by personalizing the objective for each recruiter. Rather than writing that you want an internship in the finance industry, replace it with a specific summer internship with XYZ Money Multipliers, where you can enhance your marketing skills. State the company and try to say what you would like to contribute while working there. The following is a list of objective examples, varying in specificity, but you want your objective to be as narrow as possible.

OBJECTIVES FOR INTERNSHIP

Vast *(Don't use)*
*An internship that will provide me the opportunity
to enhance my interpersonal and critical-thinking skills.*

Broad *(Avoid using)*
*An internship within the finance industry that will allow me the
opportunity to develop my financial analysis and interpersonal skills.*

Focused
An internship with XYZ Money Managers that will provide me the opportunity to develop my financial analysis and interpersonal skills.

Narrow
A summer internship in the New York City equities research division of XYZ Money Managers where I will have the opportunity to develop my financial analysis and interpersonal skills.

OBJECTIVE FOR PROSPECTIVE MENTOR

Focused, but without name
To find an individual willing to provide guidance for both the professional and personal aspects of my life.

To find an individual in the marketing segment of the film industry willing to provide guidance and support for the professional and personal aspects of my life.

OBJECTIVE FOR A PROSPECTIVE FULL-TIME POSITION

Vast *(Don't use)*
An entry-level position with a large corporation willing to provide in-depth training and a management pathway.

Broad *(Avoid using)*
A leadership role within the state legislature allowing me to deal with representatives firsthand.

Focused
An administrative position with Quick Temps Corporation leading to upper-level management.

Narrow
A full-time customer service position at the Dallas headquarters of Quix Photography, Inc. where I can help difficult customers.

THE RÉSUMÉ BODY

The goal as a prospective employee is to sell yourself to the company. The company evaluates you based on your interview (heavily) and through written documentation (résumé, application). You résumé is often the first major source of information they gather on you and can make or break your likelihood of qualifying for an interview. Your interpersonal skills can be amazing, but they have little or no benefit if your résumé keeps you from obtaining an interview.

The key to creating a successful résumé is making it "user friendly." Remember, most recruiters spend less than 30 seconds looking at your résumé even though you may have slaved over it for weeks to make it perfect.

SEVEN KEY CONCEPTS

There are seven key things necessary for a successful résumé:

1. Brevity

2. Conciseness

3. Reader-focused

4. One-page long

5. Proofreading

6. Layout (white space)

7. Eye attractors (e.g., highlighting, underlining, italics, larger type)

Avoid getting too fancy with the font! I recommend using a basic typeface like Times New Roman or Helvetica. Most fonts will work as long as they are easy to read and not script. Use a professional layout and allow your accomplishments to speak for themselves.

If you have a GPA of 3.0 or greater, put it on the résumé. If your GPA is less than that you can choose to keep it off, but its absence will cause them to ask about it early in an interview. On the flip-side, if you put that you have a 1.7 GPA on your résumé, you may not get the interview at all.

It is important to use parallel words when listing or using bullets. This means beginning each bulleted line with an action word or a noun, as long as they all begin with the same type of word. At the end of this section, you will find a list of action words that are good to use in the body of your résumé and any bulleted lists.

Depending on the position you are applying for, your résumé might be structured as follows:

1. Heading
2. Objective (optional)
3. Education
4. Work Experience
5. Achievements/Leadership/Extracurricular Activities (optional)
6. Interests (optional)
7. References (optional)

In your résumé do not include things like your height, weight, age, blood type (unless you're applying to give blood), or marital status. I would also avoid putting your salary requirements on the résumé. It looks unprofessional and in most instances salaries are negotiated after completing several interviews.

Your résumé should reflect your audience, so definitely feel free to change it for each application. For instance, if you are applying for a financial internship you might put that you interned at a bank for two months, but if you want to go into science you may replace that with a semester-long research project on photosynthesis.

ACTION WORDS

Refer to the following list of seventy-six words as you write your cover letters and résumés. Using these words helps keep your correspondence in an "active" voice rather than a "passive" voice. An active voice adds power to your résumé.

Allocate	Institute
Analyze	Instruct
Assemble	Integrate
Assist	Interpret
Balance	Interview
Budget	Maintain
Build	Manage
Calculate	Market
Collect	Monitor
Communicate	Motivate
Consolidate	Operate
Consult	Organize
Contribute	Oversee
Coordinate	Participate
Create	Perform
Delegate	Plan
Demonstrate	Prepare
Design	Present
Determine	Produce
Develop	Publicize
Direct	Recruit
Distribute	Referred
Document	Repair
Edit	Report
Establish	Represent
Evaluate	Research
Examine	Resolve
Forecast	Review
Generate	Revise
Guide	Schedule
Identify	Screen
Illustrate	Select
Implement	Supervise
Improve	Supply
Increase	Strengthen
Inform	Test
Initiate	Train
Inspect	Upgrade

Overcoming Résumé Obstacles

If you do not meet the age or other requirements for a position within a company, I recommend going to their recruiting meeting and asking a recruiter to look over your résumé for any suggestions that might help.

Tell them you realize you do not qualify for a position for whatever reason, but that you attended the meeting to learn about the company and obtain any suggestions they have about your résumé and applying to the company in the future. This way you learn ways to improve your résumé and speak with the recruiter on a more personal level. When you qualify for the position and return the next time, your résumé will be improved due to your previous effort. You also will have valuable insight into their hiring process!

Life Skills

If you feel that your résumé is still weak, the best things you can add to "beef it up" are not necessarily academic grades or work experience in the field you are pursuing. I worked on an archeological dig in the Mediterranean for one summer. This unique experience had nothing to do with the world of finance but it was the first thing that interviewers for financial positions commented on 90% of the time I interviewed. I call this *unconventional training.*

Working on the dig I learned such things as perseverance and teamwork. Recruiters look for people willing to do things "outside of the box" because they know this person sees more than just the world of finance. Remember, you are not seeking a position for just your finance knowledge, you want a position for *you.* After all, the recruiter is hiring a person, not a finance book. Being well-rounded is a definite plus.

Volunteering for something like building houses for the homeless or working to teach Spanish-speaking people English is one way to become more well-rounded. Volunteering at a hospital or interning at a finance company will be of great benefit to you as well, but sometimes it is even more beneficial to get out of the "zone" you are familiar with to gain new and different experiences.

List relevant honors, awards, jobs, etc., that have taken place within the last five years. "Relevant" in this sense means experiences that in some way present you to the potential employer in a positive light and are, even vaguely, related to the job you are seeking. Things like being an Eagle Scout should always be on your résumé, but winning third place in the agriculture division of the local science fair in sixth grade should be replaced.

If you are a college student and have not built a strong résumé, it is alright to list high school awards and achievements. However, realize that they will not have the impact of college achievements when you compete with other college students for a job. The key to an effective résumé is to give enough information to explain the activity *and* catch the reader's attention. Examples of this concept can be found in the sample résumés in this chapter.

INFORMATION OVERLOAD

So you've followed the outlines above and written down all the important information you can think of—and your résumé is ten pages long.

One of the most important things I can tell you to do is keep your résumé length to one page. Remember that recruiters spend less than 30 seconds looking at your résumé so put the information you want them to see most on one page. Even two pages can be cumbersome with the documents getting misplaced and then looking incomplete. Receiving a four-page résumé does not give the impression that the person has achieved a great deal, rather that he does not know the basics of effective self-marketing.

However, if you do decide to use a two-page résumé, do not begin the second page in the middle of a subheading. Always begin with a new section or main achievement. In other words, do not cut off the reader in the middle of your bulleted list of skills. Instead, place the entire list of skills on another page. Be sure to include a complete heading on every page of your résumé and correspondence. All your documents should look like they go together.

I started with a six-page résumé and then cut it down to one. I realized that in one page I had conveyed basically the same amount of information as I had with six pages. In the words of one of my greatest mentors, "Brevity is a virtue." If you are having trouble reducing the size of your résumé, play with the font size. In general, the font size of your résumé should stay between 10 and 14 points. Keep in mind that the smaller the type the harder it is to read, but the more you can fit onto one page.

SCANNABILITY

Scannability versus readability. What is the *scannable* résumé you often hear about when job searching? Basically, many companies (generally large ones) use computers to "scan" your résumé, looking for key words or phrases.

The easiest way to make your résumé scannable is to take out all of the methods you use to highlight information (underline, italics, etc.) in your résumé and emphasize specifics in your résumé, such as degree to be earned, achievements, and action words (see list). While the content is basically the same, the typical methods of drawing the reader's attention are not, which is fine if there is not a reader. At present, résumés are scanned a fraction of the time. The corporations that scan them are usually extremely large and receive high volumes of applications every day. If you do decide that you want a scannable résumé, I recommend not spending more than 30 minutes to alter your regular résumé to a scanner friendly one. Keep in mind that the vast majority of companies in America do not scan their résumés. If you do send a scannable résumé, be sure to include your normal résumé in the correspondence as well so you can better reach "human" readers.

For the present and near future, you should concentrate on readability, especially when you bring a copy of your résumé with you to an interview. If you are sending a cover letter and a résumé addressed "To Whom it May Concern" to a large company, scannability is something to keep in mind. There are books on scannable résumés available. If you are interested, your local library or bookstore can assist you.

Eyeing Your Résumé

Once you've typed your marketing pieces, it's time to evaluate your résumé and all accompanying material for white space, or overall eye appeal. What I recommend you do is tape the document to the wall at eye level and take two steps back. Does the layout look even? Are there any sentences that seem to just run across the page? Make sure there is a noticeable border around the document, usually one inch to one-and-a-quarter inches.

On a letter try to keep the text vertically centered on the page. If it's too high or low, space it until it fits well. It does not have to be exactly in the middle, but just enough to keep it from looking lopsided. It is all right to abbreviate such things as your state name and the word "street" for balance or space considerations, but when possible write the names fully. It again makes the letter appear more professional.

Tip: If you are using a computer to write your résumés and letters, keep a back-up disk of everything just to be extra safe.

Dressing Your Résumé

When you choose a paper for your résumé, consider all the components you are planning to send with the résumé: cover letter, business card, envelope and, afterward, a thank you card. You might want to find a paper type that has all of these options available. This way you create a unified, professional appearance with whomever you correspond.

I recommend using a nice cotton blend paper stock to dress your résumé. Find something attractive to the eye, preferably with a watermark; thick texture is not necessary. Use either white, off-white, sandstone, or light gray paper. Avoid dark colors and paper with graphics or designs, such as the popular granite background, because it makes the text difficult to read. Stay away from using bright paper as well. Although it catches people's attention, bright paper also highlights your lack of professionalism. Make sure that you use either a #10 envelope or a size that will accommodate letter-size paper without folding it down the middle.

COPY THAT RÉSUMÉ!

When making duplicates of your résumé, avoid using copy paper or regular printer paper. They look unprofessional and, for a few cents more, you can have a quality paper stock that projects professionalism. Isn't your future worth a few extra cents? Also, be sure that the entire text of your résumé copies well. Sometimes, parts of words can be cut off by inexact copying and this takes away from overall eye appeal.

SAMPLE RÉSUMÉS AND CRITIQUES

The following case studies illustrate a variety of résumé styles. Each résumé is followed by a detailed analysis explaining the mechanics of its composition. Note that the last case includes an unrevised résumé containing common errors; compare this to its revised version to see how it is strengthened. Using these résumés as models will enable you to market yourself effectively.

RÉSUMÉ CASE STUDY #1

Jordan asked me to assist him in obtaining an internship in advertising at Professional Marketers. He is a second-year student with Junior classification hours at The University of Texas at Austin. Jordan has a strong overall GPA, a solid work history, and has been involved in organizations directly related to his position. He also has strong references from his two previous jobs.

In writing his résumé we decided to include both his permanent and current address. We did this for balance and because it gives the reader an indication about where he lives outside of school. Knowing that he wanted an internship at Professional Marketers, we stated this as narrowly as possible in the objective. Jordan has a strong educational background and we elected to place this first. Besides listing the typical college information, such as overall GPA and hours of college credit, we also listed his experience with teams. This demonstrated that he has a great deal of teamwork experience that companies want.

Jordan learned that the company often hires interns for full-time positions. By listing his anticipated graduation date, he communicated that he had two summers of possible interning remaining before seeking a full-time position. Many companies like to introduce prospective full-time employees to the company through internships and co-ops at a young age. This way, they learn about the students firsthand and are better able to shape their skills and assess their capabilities. When the interns do graduate and are seeking employment, they have "experience" with the company and will not need to be trained as much as a new hire. Companies like to save money!

Jordan's last job was directly related to the one he currently desires. This experience is therefore extremely important, especially "developing advertising campaigns," which we bolded for emphasis. Hot Fire Grill is not directly related to advertising, but that experience helped him learn how to deal with customers of varying personalities and how to work under pressure.

Leadership skills can really round out a résumé. These may or may not be directly related to your intended employment, but they help develop the "person" behind the résumé. Jordan had participated in several extracurricular activities while attending college, but the three he listed promoted the image he wants to display. The first two items are related to advertising while the third is not. I feel that the third is probably the most exciting, though. Working with underprivileged youth demonstrates Jordan's compassion toward other people and his community, a definitely positive quality that employers appreciate.

Jordan ends by listing references from his last two employers. References are optional, but he feels they are strong and wants to use them to their maximum potential. He provides the reader with their names, positions, and the company's name. This allows the reader to quickly know Jordan's work relationship with them. As always, notify your references before using them!

Jordan Wayne Thomas

Current Address: Permanent Address:
23 Broghton St., Box 633   547 Jonas Lane
Austin, Texas 82623   Spring, Texas 83893
(512) 555-2764   (713) 555-7534

OBJECTIVE:
To obtain a summer internship in the advertising division of Professional Marketers.

EDUCATION:
- The University of Texas At Austin (UT)   Graduate Spring 1999
  Double major in **advertising** and psychology. Completed all basic courses. Advertising classes oriented towards team setting with a strong emphasis on interpersonal communication.
  70 credit hours   Overall GPA 3.3/4.0   Advertising GPA 3.5/4.0

WORK EXPERIENCE
- *Austin Daily Newspaper*   Summer 1996
  Intern. Assisted Director of Advertising and individual account managers with advertising themes and promotional activities. Worked extensively **developing advertising campaigns** for small businesses and assisting layout designer.

- Hot Fire Grill   Summer 1995
  Waiter. Austin barbecue restaurant with a strong local following and popular among tourists. Underwent training in dealing with customers in different situations. Learned cash register operation and gained experience working under pressure.

LEADERSHIP SKILLS
- Editor, Undergraduate Marketing Association monthly newsletter. Fall 95 - Spring 96
- Member, UT American Marketing Association and UT Undergraduate Advertising association. Fall 95 - Spring 97
- Volunteer for "Readers are Leaders," weekly tutoring program for underprivileged Austin area middle school students. Fall 96 - Spring 97

REFERENCES
- Linda Noters, Advertising Director, *Austin Daily Newspaper* (512) 555-2568
- John Arnold, Manager, Hot Fire Grill (512) 555-3534

Résumé Case Study #2

Jennifer approached me with what she felt was an absolute crisis: She needed a summer job and had no prior work experience. Jennifer and I spoke for about fifteen minutes. She believed that she did not have enough "stuff" to create a résumé. I asked her to write all of her activities and achievements for the past five years. It quickly became clear that she has had a busy high school career. She had a long list of achievements and references along with honor roll grades, but she had the misconception that résumés only include work experience. With so many extracurricular activities and academic pursuits, it is apparent Jennifer has learned how to manage her time well and has a strong work ethic. We wanted her résumé to reflect both of these attributes.

We began her résumé with a narrow objective stating exactly what position and how long she would be able to work for Brenton's Jewelry. She has no work experience, so we went with her education next. Besides listing her GPA and classification, we also tried to communicate any program and significant time-consuming activities she undertakes. This way the reader not only knows how well she does in school (grades and class rank) but also the other major things she does besides academics. We wanted to spotlight Jennifer's long list of achievements and consequently gave them a prominent place on her résumé. In Jennifer's situation, "Achievements" was a more appropriate title than "Leadership Skills" because some of the listed accomplishments were not leadership-focused.

After listing Jennifer's achievements, we listed her three strongest references. She had no work references but did have three great character references. These included her biology teacher, her pastor, and a neighbor. Although Jennifer felt that she did not have anything strong enough to put on a résumé, as you can see she did. Often listing all your activities and achievements for the last five years is a great way to start your résumé, especially if it is the first one you have ever written.

SAMPLE RÉSUMÉ #2

Jennifer Jean Sterms
3847 Oak Lane
Hearne, Texas 87344
(214) 555-1295
jsterms@internet.now

OBJECTIVE:

To gain summer employment as a frontline sales associate with Brenton's Jewelry.

EDUCATION:

- Hearne High School   Graduate Spring 1999
  - Junior in the Advanced degree program.
  - Member Hearne High School competition band.
  - Many extracurricular activities, learned valuable time management skills.
  - Three years of Spanish, moderately fluent.
  - Estimated GPA 93.4, top 25% of class.

ACHIEVEMENTS:

- First Chair flute, Hearne High School Band. Spring 1997
- Vice President, Hearne High Math Club. Fall 1996 - Spring 1997
- Vice President, Hearne High Nature Club. Fall 1995 - Spring 1996
- Member, Hearne High Writing Club. Fall 1994 - Spring 1997
- First Place, Hearne High Fiction Essay contest. Spring 1996

REFERENCES:

- Joanne King, biology teacher, Hearne High School (214) 555-2578
- Rodney Elks, pastor, First United Church of Hearne (214) 555-8629
- Janine Price, manager, Price Furniture Discounters (214) 555-2823

RÉSUMÉ CASE STUDY #3

Joshua wants a position as a sports columnist with a large newspaper. He has a strong and diverse work history that displays the many talents he possesses. He wants to express all of these qualities and promote the skills necessary for the job for which he is applying. His work history is stronger than his education, so he places work experience ahead of his education. Joshua begins with a precise objective displaying exactly the position he wants with the newspaper. This allows the reader to quickly know which position he is applying for and what to look for: writing experience and working under pressure.

His most recent job was as a weekly hockey columnist and a feature sports writer. His movement in one year from assistant columnist to feature columnist and then feature articles shows that his editor had confidence in his abilities to write and work with deadlines. Joshua's work with various sports as a feature writer is important because that is the position he is applying for at *The Los Angeles Morning Newspaper*.

Joshua's work with BRI Publishing did not include writing but did encompass editing. This is important, because in the newspaper industry, where high pressure and deadlines are everyday occurrences, any way you can reduce an editor's workload is important. His upward movement from layout designer to manager demonstrates the confidence the company felt in him. Receiving the "60 Hour" award from the company chairman demonstrates his strong work commitment and really puts him in a positive light.

Huffmann's Grill allowed Joshua to learn how to work with various types of people in sometimes stressful situations. He also moved from busboy to waiter in only one month. Joshua earned an Associate degree in literature from a junior college. With his next job centering on writing, it is important for him to note this. His GPA was solid, but his GPA in English was higher so he elected to include that as well. Joshua knows that employers often request three references, so he included three on his résumé. Including a reference from each job also shows a solid job history.

SAMPLE RÉSUMÉ #3

Joshua Smith
1232 Little Road
Hilton, Kentucky 63453
(534) 555-3524
josh_s@online.com

OBJECTIVE

To obtain a full-time position as a sports reporter for the *Los Angeles Morning Newspaper.*

PROFESSIONAL EXPERIENCE

Writers, Inc.   May 1995 - June 1996
Austin, Texas

Columnist. Wrote weekly column on college hockey along with feature articles on star players from various sports. Began as assistant columnist and advanced to columnist and feature articles in only one year. Learned to work well under extreme time deadlines.

BRI Publishing   Feb. 1994 - May 1995
Rollingwood, Texas

Editor. Oversaw all steps of book production from text to cover design. Began as layout designer and advanced to manage seven full-time employees. Received "60 Hour Week" award from company chairman for work ethic.

Huffmann's Grill   Jan. 1993 - Feb. 1994
Austin, Texas

Waiter. Worked full-time at seafood restaurant. Advanced from busboy to waiter in one month. Learned to work with different types of people in demanding situations.

EDUCATION

Barton Junior College. Associate degree in English.
3.0 overall GPA; 3.4 English GPA

REFERENCES

• Heather Frick, Chief Editor, Writers, Inc. (534) 555-3322
• Chris Stephens, Manager, book division of BRI Publishing. (534) 555- 6454
• Sharon Gilly, Manager, Huffmann's Grill. (534) 555-7636

Sample Case #4

Bryan has a steady work history with a strong background in mechanics and assembly line work. He also has some experience with management and two solid references. He has a high school diploma and no further formal education, but he did earn SE mechanic certification. Bryan wants a job as an assistant manager of an assembly line at Norvel Tooling.

It is vital that Bryan convey his extensive background in assembly work and mechanics, along with his management skills and timely promotions. Bryan has written his objective to clearly state which position with Norvel Tooling he is applying for. This objective allows the reader to quickly learn which position he desires and what type of skills to look for. Bryan begins by focusing on his work experience and then his education, as work experience is a necessity for the job he desires.

His position with Allied Tooling demonstrates hard work on his part as he was promoted from assistant to the hardware assembly manager in one year and then underwent extensive training to become an assistant manager. This shows the company believed in his abilities, because they not only promoted him but also incurred the time and expense to train him. He also displays his mastery of large machines, which will be important for managing an assembly line composed of many large machines.

Applied Assembly helps Bryan show that he does have hands-on experience with an assembly line as well an integral understanding of how engines are built. It also demonstrates work longevity, which is important if a company is going to spend the money necessary to train an employee properly. Johnson Autoworks shows that Bryan is interested in furthering his education by gaining SE certification. This position provided Bryan with management skills in the areas of bookkeeping and computers. An understanding of these skills is essential in management.

Bryan had no additional schooling past high school, but his multitude of experience really makes him a strong candidate for the position. He has also included two references from two of the three places he has worked. This makes obtaining references easy for the employers and shows Bryan's confidence in them.

SAMPLE RÉSUMÉ #4

Bryan Lorn Stephenson
2332 Altimore Road
Levingston, NY 34402
(202) 555-7786

OBJECTIVE: An assembly line assistant-manager position with Norvel Tooling.

WORK EXPERIENCE:

Allied Tooling   March 95–Jan. 97
Assistant Manager, hardware assembly. Began as assistant to hardware assembly manager. After one year underwent extensive management training and moved to assistant manager. Mastered operation of large machinery.

Applied Assembly   Feb. 90–March 95
Assembly line worker. Assembled airplane engines as well as assisted in other large engine projects. Developed hands-on skills and mastery of large engine assembly.

Johnson Autoworks   June 88–Feb. 90
Mechanic for imported cars. Worked mainly on Mercedes and Porsches. Earned SE certification and became trained expert on repairing exotic car engine problems. Also learned bookkeeping and computer-related skills.

EDUCATION:

High School Diploma
Honler High School
Class of 1988

REFERENCES:

• Jim Harverfelt, Assembly Manager, Allied Tooling, (202) 555-6649
• Ronie Jones, Foreman, Applied Assembly, (202) 555-5645

RÉSUMÉ CASE STUDY #5

Meagan approached me after several attempts to obtain a job in the highly competitive airline industry. She is twenty-two years-old and presently working as a bartender. She knew her résumé could be improved, but did not know how to strengthen it. The first thing I recommended she do was clarify and shorten her objective. The next thing was to break the monotony of the résumé by adding a line below her name. Then we removed her work phone number, because she would not be the one answering the phone and the person answering it probably does not know anything about the job she is pursuing. By including only her home number, we took away the (H) and wrote her phone number in the correct standard form (512) 555-4534. We also went back and added another space between the ZIP code and Texas. Her name fades into the background, so we enlarged it to make it stand out.

She has a great deal of experience, but does not say exactly what she learned at the job or even if she had any upward advancement. I went over with her the skills she learned along with the position where she began. Recruiters not only want to know where you worked. More importantly, they want to know what you *learned*. We did this for all of her work experience. Once we had her experience beefed-up, we went back and evaluated her education.

Meagan withdrew after one semester at UT to earn money to pay for college and has yet to return. Her GPA was less than a 3.0, so she elected to omit it on her unrevised résumé. She only took two courses at Brenn and they transferred to UT. She learned through her industry research that the company she was applying to valued work experience over education. We thus decided that it was more important to expand on her experience and work-related skills then to emphasize her short college experience.

Next, we worked on her "Special Skills" section. First, I noticed there was a spelling error. Always proofread and spell-check your work—these errors can be costly. One of the skills she had listed was ambiguous and the rest could be more "actively" explained, so we added bullets and action words.

Finally, Meagan had several strong references, so we placed two at the end to make it easy for the reader to contact them. She had her résumé on a white textured paper; I recommended she use something with a cotton blend.

SAMPLE RÉSUMÉ #5—UNREVISED

Meagan Lemmer
3425 1/2 Ave. M
Austin, TX 73534
(H) 512-555-4534
(W) 512-555-3453

Objective

To obtain a position in an Airline using my interpersonal skills, energy, and experience with the public. To use and develop my skills to assist a company in providing the best customer relations and service.

Education

The University of Texas at Austin
Austin, TX 1993-1995

Brenn College
Brenn, TX 1992

Havens High School
Havens, TX 1989-1993

Professional Experience

Mama's Bar
Austin, TX 1994-Present
Bartender

Bier Garten
Austin, TX 1995-1996
Bartender

Longmore Dental Care
Austin, TX 1993-1994
Clerical/Dental Assistant

Fultier Family Dentistry
Havens, TX 1991-1993
Clerical/Dental Assistant

Special Skills

Capable of providing security in uncomfortable situations
Able to handle customer complaints effectively
Specialize with organizational skills needed for busy office
CPR and First Aid training
Involved in the community *Mentor* program

Sample Résumé #5—Revised

Meagan Lemmer
3425 1/2 Ave. M
Austin, Texas 73534
(512) 555-4534

OBJECTIVE
To gain employment as a flight attendant with XYZ Airlines utilizing my interpersonal skills, energy, and experience dealing with customers of all backgrounds.

WORK EXPERIENCE

Mama's Bar   1994-Present
Austin, Texas
    Bartender. Began as cocktail hostess and advanced to bartender in three months. Trained in mixing drinks, dealing with unruly clients, and operating register. Extremely lively atmosphere demanding entertaining bartenders.

Bier Garten   1995-1996
Austin, Texas
    Bartender. Worked to supplement my income after withdrawing from school. Received training in mixing drinks and dealing with customers.

Longmore Dental Care   1993-1994
Austin, Texas
    Dental Assistant. Assisted dentist with patients and performed clerical work. Duties included billing insurance companies and collecting from patients.

Fultier Family Dentistry   1991-1993
Havens, Texas
    Dental Assistant. Involved in all aspects of client care. Receptionist and clerical duties along with extensive experience comforting upset children.

SKILLS
- Effectively handle customer complaints
- Experienced organizational skills within busy offices
- Active participant in community mentor program
- CPR and First Aid Certified

REFERENCES
John Clearcut, General Manager, Mama's Bar, (512) 555-7856
Rita Huenga, General Manager, Bier Garten, (512) 555-8763

FINAL RÉSUMÉ REMINDER

Your résumé does not need to include an objective or reference list; these are entirely optional and some employers prefer they are not included. If either your objective or reference list pushes your résumé over one page, delete that section rather than deleting your "selling points." One option is to list "references available upon request" near the bottom of the page, this way the potential employer knows that they are available. A good cover letter can alleviate any need for an objective; just make sure the potential employer understands which position you desire. In the end, go with what you think represents you best!!

THE ALL-IMPORTANT "THANK YOU"

It is essential that you send a thank you card immediately after meeting with anyone regarding your job search. This includes all interviews, informational meetings, and mentors. As you become more familiar with your mentor you do not need to send a thank you card, but after the initial meeting be sure to send one.

I always write my thank you cards by hand as it makes them look more personal. If you do this, be sure your handwriting is legible and does not slant up or down too much. Printing is fine, as long as it can be easily read.

Select a thank you card that is professional and conservative, the simpler the better. Try to avoid politically incorrect cards and others with messages or pictures that may convey the wrong image. Be sure to write at least one to two sentences recalling a particularly interesting or educational experience gained from the meeting. If the meeting was a job interview, insert a sentence detailing the position you desire. For example, you might write, "I enjoyed speaking with you regarding opportunities for internships in XYZ's engineering department."

Be sure the date corresponds with the wording of the thank you card. If you say "thank you for the office visit today" and have it dated the day after the office visit, it looks like you are trying to pull a fast one or did not pay close enough attention when composing the card.

Thank the person for their time and include the next step to be taken (looking forward to speaking with you next week, or I'll write you in two weeks, etc.). When signing your name, be sure that if you choose to sign "Yours truly" or "Sincerely yours" that the second word is lower case. Often people capitalize both of these. Also, avoid getting overly fancy with your signature.

A line with a loop on the end may be perceived as flashy and "unprofessional." In addition, avoid a huge signature or an extremely small one; these things both catch the reader's attention and take away from the content of the thank you card. If possible, insert your business card within the thank you card; it adds a nice professional touch.

Select a stamp that once again conveys the message you want. If at all possible, use a stamp rather than a metered stamp to pay postage. I like stamps with a conservative motif; try to avoid "Sports" and "Love" stamps. A regular first-class mail stamp with the American flag will work just fine. Place the stamp level and as well centered in the top right corner as possible—there is no reason it should be sloppily attached sideways.

This may seem like a lot of nitpicky things to keep track of, but the extra minute or so it takes to check these things will make the difference between a professional and a mediocre thank you card.

THANK YOU CARD EXAMPLES

Mr. Changelor works for Big Oil Pipeline. Josh contacted Big Oil by mail and phoned two of the employees there who directed his inquiries to Mr. Changelor. Mr. Changelor arranged for Josh to come down on a Friday. Mr. Changelor asked Rusty Welgin, his trusted employee, to organize the day for Josh.

Josh got to know Rusty pretty well and Rusty preferred that Josh call him by his first name. Mr. Changelor also asked that Josh call him by his first name but Josh did not feel too comfortable doing this. He continued calling him "Mr. Changelor."

Some people will prefer that you not call them "Mr.", "Mrs.", or "Ms.", while others will find it flattering. If, by chance, they do take offense, then address them by the name they prefer.

January 10, 1997

Dear Mr. Changelor,

Thank you again for the excellent office visit you helped orchestrate today. I appreciate the hospitality and interest you and your co-workers expressed. The books they recommended on the oil business will be helpful to my career search. I look forward to speaking with you on the 22nd about summer internships. Thank you again.

Sincerely yours,

(b-card enclosed)

Josh Edward Brigham

January 10, 1997

Dear Rusty,

I am again expressing my gratitude for the excellent office visit you organized on my behalf. Speaking with you and the other Big Oil Pipeline employees was truly a learning experience. Please express my gratitude to everyone who volunteered their time. I look forward to speaking with you in the near future.

Sincerely yours,

(b-card enclosed)

Josh Edward Brigham

Rita, an undergraduate student, was invited to attend a *Local Newspaper* company function and was the youngest person there. She spoke with Mr. Jones, recruiting officer for her school, and had the opportunity to speak with the director of human resources for *Local Newspaper*, Brandon Manner.

January 24, 1997

Dear Mr. Jones,

Thank you for inviting me to the *Local Newspaper* recruiting session this evening. I found the slide presentation informative and enjoyed speaking with Mr. Manner. I look forward to learning more about photography opportunities at *Local Newspaper* and speaking with you further at the upcoming employment fair. Thank you again.

Sincerely yours,

Rita Gonzalez

(b-card enclosed)

BUSINESS CARDS: PINT-SIZE POWER

When creating a business card there is one key thing to remember: the simpler the card, the better the impression.

The most powerful people I know have the simplest business cards. A cluttered business card shows a lack of professionalism.

Select a high-quality card stock and attractive, conservative font. Your name should be the largest font on the card and centered in the middle for distinction and eye appeal. Avoid graphics, illustrations, and neon colors.

On the card include all methods of contacting you that you want made public, i.e., mailing address, e-mail address, phone number, and voice mail number. You do not need to put student, your GPA, or your classification on the card. Before putting your e-mail address on any letterhead or business card make sure it is appropriate. Stay away from indecent addresses like *loveyou@college.edu*.

Always carry several of your business cards with you, preferably in something that will keep them from becoming mangled. Whenever you give one to someone, replace it that evening, otherwise you may run out of cards when you really need one.

JOSHUA M. SMITH

(534) 555-3524   1232 LITTLE ROAD

josh_s@online.com   HILTON, KENTUCKY 63453

LETTERS OF RECOMMENDATION

In *Step 4—Internships: Learn to Earn*, I touched upon obtaining letters of recommendation after an internship. Soliciting a letter of recommendation from a non-internship experience varies little from an internship experience. The key point for your reference to communicate is your excellent character along with specific accomplishments.

The letter of recommendation should always begin with the reference introducing him- or herself, occupation, the relationship to you, and how long the reference has been acquainted with you. Next, the reference should list some of your positive traits along with ways in which he/she feels you can benefit the company or school you are applying for.

Including a situation that illustrates one of your abilities in-depth is always good. This may be the way you saved the company a million dollars by networking all of the branches together, or the water cup recycling effort you organized to decrease the amount of company trash. Anything that places you in a positive light will work.

Your references should end the letter by allowing the recruiter the opportunity to contact them if they can be of further assistance. Usually recruiters do not contact character references unless the position entitles the applicant control over money, employees or children, or is in the medical field.

As in an internship recommendation, addressing the letter "To Whom It May Concern" is probably the easiest route. Once they write the letter, copy it and have them sign five of them for you. This way the signature is original.

If you are on exceedingly good terms with your recommendation authors, you can have them draft a letter of recommendation for you and keep it on file at their office. This way they can personalize it for every company you are applying to, but again it is almost unnecessary.

If you are uncertain about a person's willingness to write a recommendation for you, go ahead and ask him if he will. If he declines or says he just doesn't have enough time, do not worry about it and move on. Pressuring someone into writing a recommendation is unprofessional and will result in a poor recommendation.

Now that you have one reference under your belt, earn some more!

PHONE MESSAGES: REACH OUT AND IMPRESS SOMEONE

Phone impressions are important. If you are trying to reach someone and get a secretary instead, ask if it is possible to leave a voicemail message and get the direct phone number to the voice mailbox you are attempting to contact "just in case you are disconnected." This way, if you ever need to contact the person again you can skip the secretary.

This method is usually much more effective than leaving a message with the gatekeeper secretary because the person you are trying to reach usually checks voicemail several times a day. Use this method and you won't stay on the bottom of the secretary's message list anymore.

Voice mailboxes often allow you to play back your message. If this is the case, play it back to ensure that it is easily understood. Once you determine it is clear, save it and hang up. Plan on being able to leave approximately fifteen seconds worth of information.

THE PROFESSIONAL MESSAGE

Leaving a professional message is much harder than one might think. First, write down what you want to say so you have an outline of your content. This is equivalent to having an agenda ready. Practice your message several times until you become familiar with it. If at all possible, record the message on a tape recorder and play it back. Many times people are surprised by the tone or accent they take on when leaving a message, their "phone voice."

Pay particular attention to meaningless filler words, such as "uh" and "um," repetition of words, and speaking so fast that it is difficult to understand you. I recommend including some type of greeting, introducing yourself, stating the day and time, the way you met or the person who networked you, your reason for calling, your phone number, and the next step to be taken. Close with something similar to, "I'm looking forward to speaking with you in the near future," or "Have a great day."

When you place your call, make sure you do it in a place that is quiet and free from distractions. Also, have your day planner ready in case you need it.

SAMPLE MESSAGES

TO MENTOR—PREVIOUSLY CONTACTED
(beep) Hello, Mr. Berdine. This is Jason Dorsey. It is 2:25 PM on January 25th. I was calling to see if we could set a time next week to get together for about 30 minutes to follow up on the possibility of you being my mentor, as outlined in my letter of the 10th. Please call me at (343) 555-2635. I look forward to speaking with you in the near future.

TO MENTOR—NOT PREVIOUSLY CONTACTED
(I don't recommend this approach but sometimes it works better than mail.)
(beep) Mr. Johnson, it is 2:15 PM on Saturday the 25th. My name is Josh Glenn. I am an 18-year-old freshman in the business program at Colorado University. I have read a great deal about you in the Bleiberville newspaper. I am interested in the field of public relations and would like to speak with you for 10 minutes next week. Please call me at (834) 555-3343. I look forward to speaking with you soon.

REGARDING INTERNSHIP—PREVIOUSLY CONTACTED
(beep) Mrs. Britten, my name is Dennis Jackson. It is 3:45 PM on Friday the 15th. Your office received my cover letter and résumé last week and I wanted to schedule a time when we could meet to discuss internship possibilities at Big Blue Gum. Please call me at (873) 555-4353. I look forward to speaking with you soon.

REGARDING JOB—PREVIOUSLY CONTACTED
(beep) Hello, Mrs. Costanado. My name is Rachel Zeren. It is 11:05 AM on Wednesday the 25th. Your office received a cover letter and résumé from me last week. I would like to schedule an appointment for the upcoming week to discuss opportunities currently available at Bright Blue Water Park. Please contact me at (523) 555-2445. I look forward to speaking with you soon.

STEP FIVE—SELLING YOURSELF **101**

REGARDING JOB—NOT PREVIOUSLY CONTACTED (LAST RESORT)

(beep) Hello, Mr. Oldor. My name is Jenny Kollen; it is 8:45 AM on Thursday the 5th of April. I recently graduated from the University of Design with a degree in Fashion Merchandising. I am interested in full-time employment with Super Duper Dress Company. I would like to schedule a time when we can discuss opportunities available at Super Duper. Please contact me at (234) 555-2343. I look forward to speaking with you in the near future.

FAXING YOUR BEST

In case you need to send a fax to a recruiter or mentor, the following are examples of fax cover sheets. Each of these contains the pertinent information that someone will need to identify your fax and its destination. If you are sending a fax, be sure to keep the confirmation number and time. I usually call about thirty minutes later to confirm that the fax was received.

SAMPLE FAX COVER SHEET FORM

IMPORTANT FAX

PLACE OF TRANSMISSION (ALL CAPS)

phone number

FAX: fax number

To: **CONTACT in Bold and ALL CAPS**   Date: DATE FAX SENT (ALL CAPS)

Fax: (area code) fax number   Pages: #, including fax cover

From: YOUR NAME (ALL CAPS)   Phone: (area code) Your phone number

COMMENTS:

Fax for NAME AND TITLE (ALL CAPS) regarding (internship program, interview, etc.).

Please deliver to her as soon as possible. Thank you for your assistance.

(I recommend you handwrite "Thank You" and sign your name)

SAMPLE FAX COVER SHEET

IMPORTANT FAX

THE HACIENDA
(512) 555-9811
FAX: (512) 555-8003

To: **MARY TROPE**

Fax: (703) 555-4393

From: JOSHUA M. SMITH

Date: NOV. 15, 1996

Pages: 3, including fax cover

Phone: (512) 555-1244

COMMENTS:

Fax for MARY TROPE, Director of College Recruiting, Large Oil Company Summer Co-op regarding interview schedule at The University of Texas at Austin. Please deliver to her as soon as possible. Thank you for your assistance.

Thank You!!!
Joshua M. Smith

The *five* objectives for all job search correspondence are:

1.) Write to your audience.

2.) Keep it simple.

3.) Be concise.

4.) Every correspondence item is important. They are all evaluated both consciously and subconsciously when selecting potential job or mentoring candidates.

5.) *Never give up!* Persistence and consistency will enable you to get the job you want.

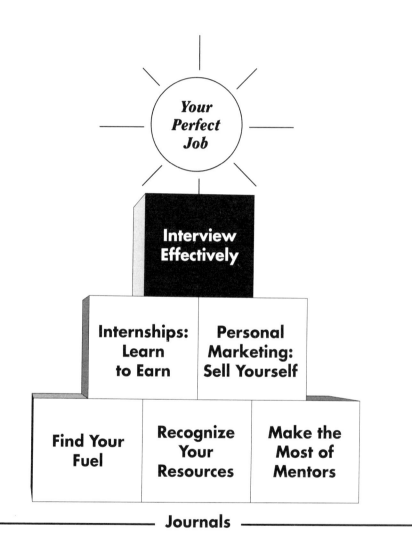

Your Perfect Job

Interview Effectively

Internships: Learn to Earn

Personal Marketing: Sell Yourself

Find Your Fuel

Recognize Your Resources

Make the Most of Mentors

Journals

Step 6
EFFECTIVE INTERVIEWING

MINDSET

Once you have successfully marketed yourself and landed the coveted interview, what now?

If you are asked to have an interview after submitting a résumé and cover letter, you probably meet the minimum requirements for the position. Keep in mind that there might be as many as 40 or 50 applicants being interviewed who have met the requirements and are equally, if not more, qualified for the position.

It is important to understand that you are probably not the most qualified person for the position. This is of small significance, because the decision of who will be hired rests heavily on the interview and the interviewer's perception of your ability to fill the vacancy. This is why the interview is often viewed as the most critical aspect of the job application process. The key thing to remember is not only how well skilled and qualified you are for the position, but *how motivated you are to work for the potential employer*. It does not matter how well qualified an employee is. If he or she has no motivation to perform a job, nothing will be accomplished and recruiters know this.

The goal of the interview is to communicate your professionalism and enthusiasm for the company to the recruiter. This is going to make the difference in who receives the job offer and who does not. In doing this, the interviewer will be evaluating your people skills, as these will indicate how much of an asset you will be in their work environment. As a highly successful HR director told me, "Jason, remember that it's *'will over skill'* every time. If you are granted an interview this generally means you have met the basic requirements for the position. The interview is an opportunity for the recruiter to determine which candidate has the most motivation to complete the job along with the interpersonal skills necessary for the workplace. The applicant hired may not be the most qualified for the job, but if she has the motivation to perform the job well, we will teach her everything she needs to know. Especially coming out of high school or college into the job world, a new hire will have to learn almost everything over. We would rather take the time to train someone who will put her full effort into the company than wasting our time with someone who is just looking for $X per hour."

INTERVIEWING: A TWO-WAY STREET

Interviewing, like networking, is a two-way street. The interviewer is trying to learn about you and you are trying to learn about her and the company. I suggest you keep generalized questions about the company to a minimum as these are usually already answered in the material they have provided. Interviewers want to you to be informed about the company when you walk in the door, as well as when you walk out. If you have studied the company, your preparation will be apparent.

Knowing not only about the company but about the particular position within the company is important. Moreover, knowing about the company does not mean memorizing the annual report, but being able to give a one-minute summary of the company and the job field of interest to you.

There are many questions routinely asked at interviews along with questions that a recruiter cannot ask. This chapter will highlight some sample questions along with things to consider when responding.

A recruiter, by law, cannot ask you questions that do not directly relate to the job being offered. This includes questions about your age, marital status, race, religion, nationality, or military service discharge. If the person does make derogatory references to any of the above, you probably would not want to work with him anyway. If you feel that you were denied the job due to discriminatory hiring practices, you can contact the appropriate government agency or organization (NAACP, NOW, your religious group, etc.).

Be aware that sometimes recruiters may "lead" applicants to determine their religion or race. An example would be, "What plans have you made for this weekend?" This may or may not be an effort to see if you are going to church, what holidays your religion observes, or if you are single.

SAMPLE QUESTIONS

The following are some frequently-asked questions. I have highlighted the important aspects recruiters look for when you respond to these questions.

1.) Who is Jason Dorsey?
This is basically an exploratory question to learn more about you, your accomplishments, and your goals. It is often the first question recruiters ask.

Tell the interviewer about your history, what you are currently doing, and what you want to accomplish in the future. Tell her a little about your personality and the way you view life. As belittling as it may seem, everyone should be able to give a short biography on themselves in one minute or less, but be prepared to go for three or four minutes if so instructed.

2.) What do you know about Big Blue Boats, Inc.?
This is where you get the chance to show off all the research you have done on the company. Tell them about the industry, how the company fits in the industry, and the position within the company that holds your interest.

3.) What position with Big Blue Boats, Inc. do you seek, and why?
This is another chance to impress them with your research. Go in-depth about your fascination with the position along with why you want it.

4.) What do you offer the company?
This is where you want to talk about your motivation, drive, enthusiasm, reliability, and skills that will increase company profits.

5.) Why do you want to work for Big Blue Boats, Inc.?
Talk about the company environment, the company's philosophy toward employees, and career advancement.

6). What are your long-term and short-term goals?
You can use the goals you constructed during the beginning of the plan to answer this question. Be honest—the sincerity will strengthen your trust with the interviewer.

7.) What experience do you have in your intended field?
Talk about your internships and the people you have shadowed, along with any mentor you have in your prospective field. If you have none, you can talk about the books you have read or any courses you may have taken.

8.) Would you like to meet some people in the department you would be working in?
Yes!! Any opportunity to learn more about the company firsthand is greatly appreciated. Employees are often the best way to learn about a company.

9.) Do you have any other questions?
Remember that list of questions you made? Use it!

AFTER THE INTERVIEW

When you leave the interview, write down your observations in your interview journal as soon as possible. This step is critical. The journal will record your progress and your thoughts on the interview. Did the interviewer have any kids or hobbies? Remembering these things the next time you meet will help to build rapport. Make sure to complete each section such as date, time, results, and the next step to be taken. Any small details that you remember should be recorded, regardless of your thoughts on their relevance. Such things as their personality and visual feedback are good to include.

A woman from Boston once interviewed me for an internship in New York City. I have friends in Boston and was familiar with the city. At our next meeting I brought this up and she was impressed I remembered. This attention to detail conveys your interest in the company and eases your anxiety.

Always follow up! At a job interview, my interviewer told me that when she received her first job in the securities industry, her interviewer decided to hire her as soon as she left the interview, but she herself did not know this. The only way the company made a job offer was if the person followed up with the recruiter within two weeks. To this day she is glad she called the next week.

If you were not hired, still contact the interviewer or the HR department and try to find out their reasons. Do not give them a hard time, but learn what you can from them. Many times you will be surprised, because often the things we do not think about were the causes, not a lack of skill. Life is all about learning. Learn from the experience so that you will be better prepared for the next opportunity you create.

JUDGING A PERSON BY FIRST IMPRESSIONS

People know only what they see and hear about you. Interviewers usually know little about you and base their judgment of your personality and potential on your interview—that is its purpose. Sure, they want to answer any questions you have, but basically it is a chance for them to get a feel for you. Realize that this is the objective of the interview and you can make it work for you. Directing your enthusiasm about the company, and why you fit both is the best approach.

In order to create a successful interview (yes, they are created), three things must be involved: preparation (mental and physical), presentation, and personality. Sharpening these three skills will allow you to have a successful interview every time.

MENTAL PREPARATION

Preparation involves everything you do prior to the meeting in order to set the best foundation possible for a productive communication session. The most important type of preparation is mental. View the upcoming meeting as an opportunity rather than a punishment for ambition. Forget the idea of the interview as an interrogation by an overweight man in a smoky room with a bright light firing questions at you. Replace it with two people sitting down in an office to engage in a mutually beneficial conversation.

The key is to enter the meeting/interview with the mindset that each person in the conversation is present in order to gain better insight into the other person. Meetings are give-and-take. Do not let the interviewer's position intimidate you. She is just another person already hired by the company with the job responsibility of finding other motivated and talented people to join her and the company in moving forward.

Once you begin to view the interview as a meeting, it will begin to feel more comfortable. Removing the interrogation feeling from the interview allows you to focus on your goal of positively representing yourself and your importance to the company. An interview should reveal more about the company, its employees, its goals, and where you fit in its equation for success.

MEMORIZING THE MISSION STATEMENT

If you have the chance to memorize the company's *mission statement* or *vision statement*—or whatever it labels its core beliefs—do so. When the recruiter asks you what you know about the company, imagine the impact of responding, "XYZ Credit Company is a diversified corporate lending and investment company with 420 branches and 12 billion dollars in revenue. Its mission statement is to. . ." Wow, talk about blowing an interviewer away! They will know you are serious about the job because you learned their mission statement and company culture. Keep working that mental muscle into shape so that you can enter the meeting room ready to put your best foot and attitude forward.

IF YOU DREAM IT, YOU CAN ACHIEVE IT

Many top sports players and other professionals use mental visualization to enhance their performance. They imagine making the winning shot, crossing the finish line first, or landing the deal that gets their face on the cover of *The Wall Street Journal*.

If you are extremely nervous about the upcoming interview, visualize a positive interviewing experience. Imagine yourself talking confidently with your interviewer. I also recommend imagining a place where you would feel safe if money and time were of no importance. If you feel nervous during the interview, visualize this place and remember that performing well during the interview will get you one step closer to reaching this goal.

AGENDA MANIA

As mentioned in Step 3, always bring an agenda to the meeting, whether it is an interview or a mentor meeting. This agenda serves many purposes. Foremost, it reminds you of the topics you intend to cover but allows you enough flexibility to go with the flow of the conversation. Agendas set the tone for the meeting and allow their creator to greatly influence the direction of the meeting. It is not necessary to disclose your agenda to the interviewer, but I do recommend writing it down and keeping it where it is easily accessible during the interview.

You don't have to stick with topics that deal strictly with the potential employer. In fact, I like to vary the topics beginning with the company, the interviewer, and marketing myself. Varied topics will allow you to assemble a better picture of the company and the interviewer along with assisting in building rapport by speaking to the interviewer on a slightly more personal basis.

Included in the agenda should be a list of questions you prepared ahead of time about the company, interviewer, industry, and your place within the big picture. This shows you have researched the company thoroughly along with your strong desire to obtain the job. Avoid or limit general questions and stick with more personal ones such as:

- *What do you look for in an applicant for this position?*
- *Why did you initially choose to work for XYZ Super Market?*
- *What do you like most about your job?*
- *What do you like least about your job?*
- *How stressful is the work environment?*
- *Have you noticed changes in the company since you began working here?*
- *Do you view the company as being a place where someone can work for 5 or more years?*

- *What kind of career advancement opportunities are available?*

- *How long have you been with the company?*

- *Did you work anywhere before starting here?*

- *Is there anything I should know about the job that I didn't ask?*

The key is to customize your questions to your interviewer and their background. What is the interviewer's gender and ethnic background? What do you have in common with them? Did you contact them? Have they been interviewing people all day? Are you over- or underqualified for the position? What can you do to stand out among the other candidates? Notice the setting of the meeting. Is it casual, such as a coffeehouse, or is it formal, such as an office visit?

Shape your interview anxiety into fuel for your enthusiasm. Learn to make your nervousness work for you. Get excited about job interviews and the possibility of meeting someone new. If you do not seize the opportunity to apply for a job and take the chance of being turned down, you never have a chance of getting the job. Speak from your heart. Remember, *you can do it if you believe in yourself!*

PHYSICAL PREPARATION

First impressions, especially physical impressions, are critical to the interviewer's initial assessment of you. Within the 30 seconds after first meeting the interviewer, numerous assumptions about you have already been made. Stereotyping may not be politically correct, but it is a reality during the job interview. What impression would you have if someone walked in to get a job from you wearing an untucked T-shirt, hat hair, unshaven, and without the best body odor? In the white-collar world there is a good chance that the person would not gain employment based on his appearance alone, because employees represent the company and that is not the professional representation the company wants.

Appearing clean and respectfully dressed provides the best background for the interviewer to focus on your non-physical attributes, not what you are wearing, but who you are. A good friend of mine who has done a great deal of hiring told me, "When you leave an interview, you do not want to be remembered for your hair, cologne, shoes, shirt, tie, or jewelry. If the person remembers you for your physical appearance, you have done an average interview, exactly what the majority of applicants I see do. When you leave that room you want to be remembered for your personality, knowledge, interest, enthusiasm, courtesy, and motivation. You want them to remember *you*." Keep this in mind when going into an interview and you will make the impression you want.

CREATING THE BACKGROUND

The way you create this professional impression is by dressing for your audience and arriving prepared and 15 minutes early. Your agenda for the meeting is already written. I strongly recommend you iron/steam your outfit and hang it up the night before; it is one less thing to worry about the day of your interview. Make sure that your clothes are clean!

As a rule, it is better to overdress than to underdress. Women have the option of wearing a skirt and blouse or some type of conservative outfit geared toward a suit feeling. Women should avoid skirts and blouses with a little girl or romantic feel to them. Also stay away from big, lacy collars or embroidery in different color thread. The ideal blouse is simple, starched, and white; the ideal skirt would be a suit skirt with straight lines and very clean in design, black or navy. I recommend a hemline no higher than three inches above the center of the knee. You want to seem professional and non-intimidating, especially if your interviewer is a woman. If you do not have an outfit that fits this description, borrow something from your friends or religious group.

Footwear is important for women. Avoid open-toed shoes and wear panty hose, sheer black or natural, depending on your skirt/suit choice. If you are only going to buy one pair of shoes, buy black, smooth-grained leather with no buckles or metal of any sort. Black goes with everything, including a navy skirt. You do not want your shoes to limit you. Avoid uncomfortable shoes, because you may be touring the company. I recommend shoes with an approximately 1½-inch heel and in a "chunky wedge," if possible, not tapered. Most shoe stores will be able to explain this in more detail.

Professionalism is important to both genders. Men should wear a suit if possible, or dress pants and a tie. Men should always wear a tie, knotted in something besides a slip knot, if possible, preferably the Half Windsor (see illustration). Any knot is fine, but avoid both very small and very large knots. Your tie should touch the tip of your belt buckle. It takes some practice, but when you get the length right once, it is easy repeat next time. When selecting a tie to wear, there are a few things to keep in mind. Is the business very conservative, like banking? Is it more casual, such as an upstart Internet company where the CEO wears jeans? Dress to fit the company image!

1. Take A, which is longer and wider than B, and cross it over B.

2. Bring A around and behind B.

3. Then bring A up.

4. And put A back through the loop.

5. Now bring A back over B.

6. And once more bring A up through the loop.

7. Bring A down through the outer loop in front.

8. Tighten the knot with both hands.

How to tie a Half Windsor Knot

In general, business is a conservative industry and I recommend you stick with a conservative tie and outfit. Remember, the CEO wearing jeans already has a job (and sets the dress code). Conservative implies something besides a cartoon and loud colors—something simple and professional. You want the interviewer to remember you for your enthusiasm, not your tie. Some businesspeople I know firmly adhere to the belief that a tie represents your personality. I do not fully agree with this, but I know that the feeling the tie evokes is reflected upon its wearer. Do not wear offensive ties; these include ties with pictures that are graphic or cartoons with inappropriate language.

When selecting shoes, men should look for something with a light shine. I recommend both men and women invest in shoe polish and shine their shoes before an interview. Men, if buying only one pair of shoes, should choose black or chocolate colors and lace-ups over loafers. Your belt should obviously match your shoes in both texture and color.

If you are considering buying two pairs of shoes, I recommend buying one nice pair. One nice pair of shoes looks much better than two "OK" pairs. Take good care of your dress shoes and they will look good for a long time.

When selecting a shirt, men should keep the one versus two philosophy in mind. Look for a shirt that is lightweight and long sleeve, but is thick enough so that you cannot see right through it (keep your undershirt to yourself). Have your shirt pressed at the cleaners or starched heavily. I always make sure to starch the pocket so that it does not sag. I also starch my collar heavily; otherwise it wrinkles when you knot your tie. A successful business owner showed me a trick he learned as a child watching his neighbors iron clothes for a living in his native country. Basically, you starch the collar heavily from behind and then fold it over. It is quick, effective, and looks good.

If the interview room has a coat rack, hang your jacket on it. If not, lay your jacket over a chair. The better you take care of your professional clothes, the longer they will last.

Oh, De Toilet!!

Men and women should both avoid wearing too much cologne! Many of the interviewers I spoke with went as far as to suggest wearing no cologne at all. Deodorant and a good shower will work in most cases. People too often become adjusted to their cologne and put on way too much, especially if they are nervous. Do not suffocate your interviewer!

Before going to the interview, brush your teeth and use some type of mouthwash. You are going to be talking with someone you probably do not know for at least 30 minutes—bad breath will greatly stress the situation. Do not eat colored candy or purple passion punch gum. Sure, they help your breath, but they also turn your teeth funky colors. Try some type of white mint, a little breath spray, or white colored gum. Be sure if you are chewing gum you dispose of it before the interview. It is difficult and unprofessional to chew gum and engage in a professional conversation.

While interviewing, you will likely use some form of hand gestures, so clean and trim your fingernails before the interview. For women, I recommend polishing your nails with a clear or semi-clear color or French manicure; avoid loud or dark colors for your interview. Once again, you want your nails to not be a centerpiece of attention.

NO NEED FOR FIVE-CARAT DIAMONDS

Wear little or no jewelry. For men, I recommend wearing a watch and possibly one ring (maybe your class ring). Women can wear more than one ring, but keep the jewelry you wear to an absolute minimum. Do not wear bracelets, dangling earrings, and necklaces with charms or pendants. A simple chain is okay, but if it interferes with your shirt collar or does not lie flat, skip it. Hoop earrings are okay if they are tiny and close to the ear. All of the above have the potential to move when you talk or gesture, which distracts from what you are saying.

Both men and women should try to match all the metals in their outfit, including their belt buckle, watch, earrings, and rings. Go "all gold" or "all silver." If a piece of your "jewelry" is two-tone, select one of its "colors" and arrange the rest of your pieces around it.

INTERVIEWING MATERIALS

There are several things you should take with you to the interview. The most important are directions to get to the company, a company contact phone number, your agenda, pens, paper, *three* copies of your résumé, *three* references, and your day planner (if you don't have one, get one). The easiest way to carry these things is in some type of folder or organizer. I recommend using the folder I described in *Step 2*, because it will hold everything you need. I strongly recommend investing in two nice-looking pens. I realize they can get expensive, so most professional-looking pens will suffice. Make sure they have lots of ink left in them before you take them to the interview. Leave the "freebie" career fair pens at home!

Obtain the directions to the place you are going at least three days ahead of time. This allows you to drive there before the meeting and get familiar with the area. When I have a meeting arranged at a place I have never been, I drive there a few days before and as close to the time of the meeting as possible. This way I can record the time it takes me to get there and plan accordingly for the day of the meeting.

Take into account such things as the time of the day you will be driving and the amount of traffic. Make note of school zones and other areas where driving speed is reduced at certain times of day; this can increase your commute. Also, if the person you are meeting asks if you had any trouble finding the building, tell them you drove there the day before so you could determine the amount of time it would take to get there—it shows preparation.

Once you have the directions, file them with other data on that company in your *My Perfect Job*™ Company Research Journal. This saves you the time of having to call again and they may be impressed that you were so resourceful.

Arrive at the interview at least fifteen minutes early. If you are parking in a building garage and are given a time ticket, be sure to bring it with you to the interview so you can have the receptionist validate it. This is a common courtesy extended by most companies and will save you money.

As soon as you arrive, go to the restroom and do a final check using the *My Perfect Job*™ Pre-Meeting Checklist to make sure that you look professional. Announce yourself to the secretary about five to ten minutes early. It always looks professional to arrive early and the extra time provides a cushion if you are caught unexpectedly in traffic.

TOO LITTLE TIME??

After figuring the maximum amount of time to set aside for the meeting, add an extra half hour. This way, if the meeting is going well and it runs over, you can stay. The extra time might be crucial for you to clinch the job.

PRACTICE MAKES PERFECT (OR AT LEAST "BETTER")

An excellent way to improve your interviewing skills is to take part in a practice interview. Make the setting as real as possible so you can gain some familiarity with the interview environment. I prefer to work with professionals in the career field I want to enter, because they are more familiar with the job I want and can add personal insight after already going through the interviewing process themselves.

The Career Services Office and other school resources often host practice interview sessions. Use these opportunities to sharpen your skills. I do not recommend practicing with friends because it might be difficult to take the practice seriously. Pay particular attention to your use of eye contact and filler words. It is your future you're working for—practice makes it achievable.

Have the interviewer write down feedback after the practice interview and then have him/her go over it with you. People tend to be defensive when hearing criticism, so it helps to take their comments home with you so you can review them in a more comfortable environment. Write down the results of your practice interviews in your *My Perfect Job*™ Interview Journal.

MY PERFECT JOB™ PRE-MEETING CHECKLIST

- ❑ Check teeth for post-meal snacks
- ❑ Check nose for any unwanted guests
- ❑ Check shirt for any food or other debris
- ❑ Check tie for length
- ❑ Zipper up to succeed
- ❑ Check for lipstick on teeth
- ❑ Check skirt for wrinkles
- ❑ Fingernails trimmed and cleaned
- ❑ Hands washed
- ❑ Check for shaving cream under chin or behind ears
- ❑ Check for eye residue (yuck!)
- ❑ Check for eye makeup smears
- ❑ Tuck in shirt, front and back
- ❑ Check front of clothes
- ❑ Check back of clothes
- ❑ Belt through all belt loops
- ❑ Shoes shined
- ❑ Nothing clinging to shoes
- ❑ Wear little or no cologne
- ❑ Wristwatch
- ❑ Résumés–(3)
- ❑ Business cards
- ❑ Nice pens–(2)
- ❑ Notepad
- ❑ Directions to destination
- ❑ Be excited!!!!

SHAKE HANDS FIRMLY!!!!

At the beginning and end of the interview, you should always shake the interviewer's hand, no matter how you think the interview has gone. When you do this, be sure to give a firm handshake (but don't try to break their hand, because it's not arm wrestling!).

There is a common misconception that women should not shake hands firmly. This is completely wrong. Regardless of gender, a firm handshake begins and ends the meeting on a positive and professional note.

I remember the people who have weak handshakes, because it feels as if you are shaking a limp fish. When you are shaking the person's hand, look him/her in the eye and make sure you say your name clearly. Shaking someone's hand and looking at the ground creates the impression that you feel unworthy or insecure.

UNCOMMON COURTESY

Do not interrupt when the interviewer is speaking to you. In some instances, such as when you are with friends, doing so might be fine. Regardless, show courtesy throughout the interview by allowing the interviewer to speak. Sometimes interviewers will pause or in some way indicate that they are awaiting your reply. Most often, the communication is in a more relaxed, conversational format where the speakers will periodically exchange ideas. The *best communicators* are the *best listeners!*

DISPLAY THE POSITIVES

Focus on your strengths and not your weaknesses. Allow your enthusiasm to overcome your lack of experience or advanced degree. If you have an opportunity to tour the facility with the interviewer, do your best not to look at the ground (unless applying to a flooring company). Always looking down shows insecurity, and most people do not even realize they do it.

REMINDERS

If you catch yourself saying filler words such as "umm" and "uhh," replace them with a pause instead. There is no reason to bring a pager or cell phone to the meeting, so leave your electronics in your car. It looks plain tacky to walk in with a cell phone strapped to your belt or a pager hanging out of your pocket. It is not as impressive as the advertisers want you to believe.

If you must keep your cell phone or pager with you, keep it hidden and put it on "silent." Before leaving, make sure to obtain the interviewer's business card or write down his name, title, address, phone number, and e-mail. Many times, names are not spelled as they sound, so be sure you obtain the correct spelling before writing a thank you card.

COMMUNICATING WITHOUT WORDS

Researchers estimate the vast majority of communication is nonverbal or "unsaid." This does not mean that what you are saying is unimportant, rather it suggests you should be very aware of what your body is saying about you. Nonverbal communication includes your posture, eye contact, biting your fingernails, and moving around in your chair. Each of these things can greatly help or hurt the interview session.

One of the most annoying things is when you are talking to someone and they are looking at something else. In an interview it shows lack of interest and professionalism if you do not look at the interviewer. Also avoid crossing your arms, especially when seated, as it is perceived to be a defensive position and interviewers know this. It shows that either you are uncomfortable or unsure of your answers.

Communicate confidence by leaving your hands either at your side or in your lap, somewhere easily accessible for polite gestures. Keep them off your chest and out of your pockets as much as possible. Do your best to not to slouch in your chair. Carry yourself in a way that shows your confidence. Regardless of how comfortable you get with the interviewer, do not put your feet on their desk or on another chair (no matter how much you like those new heels).

HEARING THE UNSAID

Look for visual hints such as smiling and physical responses to your questions. These can tell you more about the answer than the actual words. For example, if you ask the interviewer about the financial stability of the company and he/she starts fidgeting or looks up at the ceiling while answering, the job might not be as permanent a position as you'd like.

Your delivery should be *confident and enthusiastic*. Demonstrating these two traits alone will separate you from many of the other applicants. There is no need to be a talking statue during your interview. Just relax and let your enthusiasm and confidence flow.

Good communication skills are essential to getting a job in today's market. Avoid words and phrases that demonstrate insecurity, such as "Hopefully," "Possibly," or "If I get the chance." Use words that show your confidence, such as "I can" and "I will." This is important for all aspects of communication, whether it's written, communicated over the telephone, or said facet . If you want to get a professional job, practice communicating like a professional.

RECRUITING YOUR TASTEBUDS

Companies often take potential employees to eat in order to gain a better feel for them in a relaxed environment. This is a great opportunity to learn more about a potential employer. In this environment you might feel more comfortable asking additional questions that weren't answered during the interview.

OUCH!! PAYING THE BILL

If a company takes you out to eat, do not ask whether or not they are paying. Bring enough cash with you to cover your meal but assume that they are going to pay for your food. Do not appear shocked or offended when the interviewer picks up the bill. You are worth the price of a good meal! Keep in mind that they are the ones recruiting you.

If you are meeting with a mentor or conducting an informational interview, I recommend paying for their food. Unless they really oppose your show of gratitude for their time, pay the bill. They may refuse and even insist on paying for your food. If they do, let them. Make sure, though, that you have enough money to pay for the bill in case they imply that you should pay. It is not that they are cheap, but rather that you invited them, and they are taking time out of their schedule for you. This has never happened to me, but I try to pay for my mentors as often as possible. If this bothers you, meet someplace where the bill will not be very high—this makes it easier for everyone.

IMITATING A COW

There are several things to keep in mind that will make the meeting go much smoother when you eat with an interviewer, businessperson, or mentor.

Do your best to take manageable bites of food, the smaller the better. The key is to not shove half a prime rib (or a head of lettuce, for vegetarians) in your mouth at once. If you do, you'll look like a cow!

Remember, taking small bites is more than just good manners, it also makes it easier to carry on a conversation. This may not seem too difficult, but just try to carry on a professional conversation while taking big mouthfuls of food! While you keep having to stop so you can chew, everyone will sit there, waiting for you to answer, focusing on your cheeks bulging like a squirrel, as sweat trickles down your forehead. Avoid this situation by taking smaller bites of food.

NO SPAGHETTI??

When ordering food, there are a few key considerations to keep in mind. Avoid ordering messy or time-consuming food. By this I mean stringy pasta, soups, and overflowing hamburgers. Regardless of your age and what the interviewer does, do not consume alcohol. They may drink a beer to see if you will order one as well, but the "three-martini lunches" are no longer the norm for conducting business. Who wants to hire someone who drinks during lunch? For all they know you may return to work drunk every day, greatly diminishing your value to the company after 1:00 PM.

Do your best to eat everything you order. The company is paying for you, so avoid wasting food. Not finishing your broccoli is one thing; not finishing all of your courses may be interpreted as you being wasteful. Just be conscious of this. Before eating, go to the restroom to wash your hands. I recommend that you even tell them this. Good hygiene is a definite plus. While in the restroom do another quick interview check to make sure that you look alright. If at all possible, do not spend long amounts of time in the restroom. What would you think if you took someone to lunch and they spent ten minutes in the restroom? Immodium A-D?

When you finish your meal go to the restroom and do a quick interview check. Pay careful attention to your shirt, tie, and teeth. The only good way to take food with you is in a doggy bag, not on your clothes.

MANNERS, MANNERS, AND MORE MANNERS

Eventually, one of the interviewers will ask you a question while you are chewing. If you are chewing a small amount of food, you can answer or signal that you need a moment, and then begin your reply. This cuts down on "dead time" in the conversation and eases the tension you may be experiencing, making the lunch more comfortable for you. You probably have been told not to smack, especially when you were a kid. For once, listen to your elders and chew with your mouth closed! Also put your napkin in your lap when the appetizers arrive and avoid slurping when you drink.

Act courteously to everyone who helps you, whether they are the restaurant manager, hostess, waitperson, or busboy. Why is this important? This extension of courtesy presents a positive image of your manners and shows that you respect people regardless of position and title. This demonstrates that you deal well with diversity and are a real team-player, increasing your value to the company.

During the meal, there may be a lull in the conversation where everyone is looking at each other trying to think of something to say. Try renewing the conversation by commenting on a noncontroversial topic of the day. Keep away from sensitive subjects such as money, gender, politics, and especially religion. This is a business meeting after all.

You can say something such as, "Did you see the ending of lasts night's baseball game? It was a real nail-biter." Even if the person is not a baseball fan she may reply by talking about another sport or hobby she likes. Another option is to say something more personal: "I heard on the news today that the weather is supposed to be excellent this weekend. I am taking my nephew to the park, do you have any plans?" This may be a bit personal, but if the rapport is building, and if the person has plans, it can be an excellent question to get the conversation flowing again and strengthen the relationship. Be sure to make mental notes of any hobbies or other important details she mentions, so you can bring them up next time you meet.

Conversations are too often power struggles, but they do not have to be. View the meal meeting as a knowledge-gathering session. If you are commenting on a sensitive subject do your best to act open-minded rather than taking opposite sides. A negative criticism can ruin a good meeting. A sensitive issue should not be discussed in the first place, but being open-minded also displays your desire to make an informed decision. This quality is essential in the business world.

SALT WITH THAT STEAK?

I heard about a company near Dallas, Texas, that has a unique way of screening applicants for its top executive positions. The board takes the applicant to dinner, making sure the applicant has never eaten at the restaurant before. If the applicant salts his food before tasting it, they believe he is stuck in his ways and will not be as responsive to new ideas and changes as someone who tastes his meal before deciding to add salt or pepper. I do not know how true the "salt test" theory is, but I suggest you taste your food before you salt it. Enjoy the meal and the opportunity!!

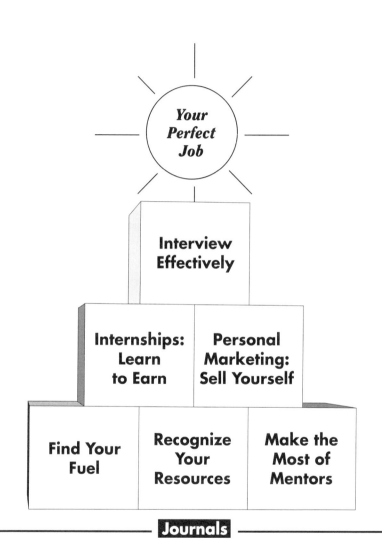

JOURNALS:
WRITE IT DOWN OR FORGET IT!

The journals on the following pages will be extremely helpful in optimizing your job search. Documenting your research and observations is the best way to keep track of your progress. The journals will also provide interesting reading when you look back at how far you have advanced with your career. Keep following your heart and never give up!!!!

INDUSTRY RESEARCH JOURNAL

Industry Name: _____

Industry Description: _____

Dominant Companies in Past: _____

Dominant Companies in Future (likely): _____

Industry growing or downsizing? _____

Public perception of industry: _____

_____

TRADE OR INDUSTRY JOURNALS

Title/Issue: _____

Comments: _____

_____

_____

Title/Issue: _____

Comments: _____

_____

_____

Title/Issue: _____

Comments: _____

_____

_____

BUSINESS PUBLICATIONS

Title/Issue: _____

Comments: _____

_____

_____

Title/Issue: _____

Comments: _____

_____

_____

Title/Issue: _____

Comments: _____

_____

_____

1/2

INDUSTRY CONTACTS

Name: _____

Title: _____

Company: _____

Address: _____

Phone: _____

Fax: _____

E-mail: _____

Name: _____

Title: _____

Company: _____

Address: _____

Phone: _____

Fax: _____

E-mail: _____

Name: _____

Title: _____

Company: _____

Address: _____

Phone: _____

Fax: _____

E-mail: _____

Name: _____

Title: _____

Company: _____

Address: _____

Phone: _____

Fax: _____

E-mail: _____

2/2

MY PERFECT JOB™ COMPANY RESEARCH JOURNAL

Company: _____

Industry: _____

Company History: _____

Future: _____

Five Sentence Company Summary:

_____

_____

_____

_____

_____

CONTACT PERSON

Name: _____

Title: _____

Company: _____

Address: _____

Phone: _____

Fax: _____

E-mail: _____

My Perfect Job™ Communication Record

Date Sent: _____

Addressee's Name: _____

Title: _____

Company: _____

METHOD OF COMMUNICATION:

      ❏ Letter   ❏ Fax   ❏ Phone   ❏ E-mail

Purpose: _____

Next Step: _____

If Phone Message:

Time of call: _____ : _____ AM/PM

❏ Person contacted
❏ Left Message with secretary
❏ Voice Mail or Recorder

If Mail Communication:

Certified Mail#: _____

Date return card received: _____ / _____ / _____

If Fax Communication:

Time of fax: _____ : _____ AM/PM

Confirmation #: _____

If E-mail Communication:

❏ Accepted
❏ Verification of letter reception

MY PERFECT JOB™ INTERVIEW JOURNAL

Date: _____

Name: _____

Title: _____

Company: _____

Address: _____

Phone: _____

Fax: _____

E-mail: _____

MEETING

Length:_____

Topics Covered (summary of each):

1. _____

_____

2. _____

_____

3. _____

_____

4. _____

_____

5. _____

_____

6. _____

_____

7. _____

_____

8. _____

_____

9. _____

_____

10. _____

_____

Answers to prepared questions:

1. _____

2. _____

3. _____

4. _____

5. _____

6. _____

7. _____

8. _____

9. _____

10. _____

Miscellaneous Comments (*e.g., kids, hobbies, etc.*):

_____

_____

_____

_____

_____

Next Step: _____

THANK YOU CARD:

Date Sent: _____

MY PERFECT JOB™ INTERNSHIP JOURNAL

Date: _____

Company: _____

Comments: _____

_____

_____

_____

_____

Books Recommended: _____

By: _____

Magazines Recommended: _____

By: _____

Contacts Recommended: _____

By: _____

Date: _____

Company: _____

Comments: _____

_____

_____

_____

_____

Books Recommended: _____

_____

By: _____

Magazines Recommended: _____

_____

By: _____

Contacts Recommended: _____

_____

By: _____

Date: _____

Company: _____

Comments: _____

_____

_____

_____

_____

Books Recommended: _____

By: _____

Magazines Recommended: _____

By: _____

Contacts Recommended: _____

By: _____

Date: _____

Company: _____

Comments: _____

_____

_____

_____

_____

Books Recommended: _____

_____

By: _____

Magazines Recommended: _____

_____

By: _____

Contacts Recommended: _____

_____

By: _____

Our Innovative Resources Can Help You and Your Organization!

Golden Ladder Productions, Ltd. is committed to helping individuals and organizations reach their goals. We offer the following education resources at volume discounts through Academic Superstore.

50 WAYS TO IMPROVE SCHOOLS FOR UNDER $50

QTY.	UNIT COST	
1-49	12.95	*Recommended by*
50-499	11.95	*school improvement*
500-999	9.95	*leaders!*
1000-5000	7.95	
5001+	6.95	*(45% off cover price!)*

My Reality Check Bounced!

QTY.	UNIT COST	
1-49	14.00	*Featured on*
50-499	12.50	*60 Minutes, 20/20*
500-999	11.00	*and in Fortune*
1000+	9.50	*Magazine!*

Graduate to Your Perfect Job

QTY.	UNIT COST	
1-49	14.95	*National bestseller!*
50-499	11.00	
500-999	10.00	
1000+	7.50	
Class Set*	349.00	*(Save over $150!)*

Graduate to Your Perfect Job—Teacher's Curriculum

QTY.	UNIT COST	
1 or more	35.00	
Class Set*	349.00	*(Save over $150!)*

* Each class set includes thirty (30) Graduate to Your Perfect Job books and one (1) Teacher's Curriculum.

Please refer to this price list when ordering Jason Dorsey's materials from Academic Superstore. You can contact Academic Superstore online at **www.AcademicSuperstore.com/JasonDorsey** or toll free at **(866) 299-6887**. Thank you for sharing Jason's inspiring message!

JASON DORSEY RESOURCE ORDER FORM
c/o ACADEMIC SUPERSTORE

NAME   TITLE

ORGANIZATION

MAILING ADDRESS

CITY   STATE   POSTAL CODE

BILLING ADDRESS (IF DIFFERENT THAN ABOVE)

CITY   STATE   POSTAL CODE

WORK PHONE   WORK E-MAIL

Payment Options

PURCHASE ORDER #   (PLEASE ATTACH PURCHASE ORDER TO THIS ORDER FORM.)

CHECK #   (PAYABLE TO ACADEMIC SUPERSTORE)

ITEM	QTY	UNIT COST	AMOUNT
50 Ways to Improve Schools			
Graduate to Your Perfect Job			
Graduate to Your Perfect Job–Teacher's Curriculum			
Graduate to Your Perfect Job–Class Set			
My Reality Check Bounced!			

Subtotal _____

Shipping [add 7% ($4.95 min.)] _____

Total _____

Mail or Fax Your Order to:

Academic Superstore 2101 E. Saint Elmo Road, Suite 360 Austin, Texas 78744	Phone: (866) 299-6887 Fax: (866) 947-4604 Contact@AcademicSuperstore.com

To request a free DVD of Jason's most popular presentations visit **www.JasonDorsey.com**

Our Innovative Resources Can Help You and Your Organization!

Golden Ladder Productions, Ltd. is committed to helping individuals and organizations reach their goals. We offer the following education resources at volume discounts through Academic Superstore.

50 WAYS TO IMPROVE SCHOOLS FOR UNDER $50

QTY.	UNIT COST	
1-49	12.95	*Recommended by*
50-499	11.95	*school improvement*
500-999	9.95	*leaders!*
1000-5000	7.95	
5001+	6.95	*(45% off cover price!)*

My Reality Check Bounced!

QTY.	UNIT COST	
1-49	14.00	*Featured on*
50-499	12.50	*60 Minutes, 20/20*
500-999	11.00	*and in Fortune*
1000+	9.50	*Magazine!*

Graduate to Your Perfect Job

QTY.	UNIT COST	
1-49	14.95	*National bestseller!*
50-499	11.00	
500-999	10.00	
1000+	7.50	
Class Set*	349.00	*(Save over $150!)*

Graduate to Your Perfect Job—Teacher's Curriculum

QTY.	UNIT COST	
1 or more	35.00	
Class Set*	349.00	*(Save over $150!)*

* *Each class set includes thirty (30) Graduate to Your Perfect Job books and one (1) Teacher's Curriculum.*

Please refer to this price list when ordering Jason Dorsey's materials from Academic Superstore. You can contact Academic Superstore online at **www.AcademicSuperstore.com/JasonDorsey** or toll free at **(866) 299-6887**. Thank you for sharing Jason's inspiring message!

JASON DORSEY RESOURCE ORDER FORM
c/o ACADEMIC SUPERSTORE

NAME   TITLE

ORGANIZATION

MAILING ADDRESS

CITY   STATE   POSTAL CODE

BILLING ADDRESS (IF DIFFERENT THAN ABOVE)

CITY   STATE   POSTAL CODE

WORK PHONE   WORK E-MAIL

Payment Options

PURCHASE ORDER #   (PLEASE ATTACH PURCHASE ORDER TO THIS ORDER FORM.)

CHECK #   (PAYABLE TO ACADEMIC SUPERSTORE)

ITEM	QTY	UNIT COST	AMOUNT
50 Ways to Improve Schools			
Graduate to Your Perfect Job			
Graduate to Your Perfect Job–Teacher's Curriculum			
Graduate to Your Perfect Job–Class Set			
My Reality Check Bounced!			

Subtotal _____

Shipping [add 7% ($4.95 min.)] _____

Total _____

Mail or Fax Your Order to:	
Academic Superstore 2101 E. Saint Elmo Road, Suite 360 Austin, Texas 78744	Phone: (866) 299-6887 Fax: (866) 947-4604 Contact@AcademicSuperstore.com

To request a free DVD of Jason's most popular presentations visit **www.JasonDorsey.com**

Dear Reader,

When you finish this book, *please* pass it on to a friend. You never know how many lives you impact when you share a book!

Your friend,

Jason R. Dorsey